Giving Wings to the Soul

Giving Wings to the Soul

DENNIS NGIEN

WIPF & STOCK · Eugene, Oregon

GIVING WINGS TO THE SOUL

Wipf & Stock
An Imprint of Wipf and Stock Publishers
199 W. 8th Ave., Suite 3
Eugene, OR 97401
www.wipfandstock.com

ISBN 13: 978-1-61097-099-0

Manufactured in the U.S.A.

In Loving Memory of
the Late Madam Ngu Poh Teh,
My beloved Mother,
Whose wish to be in Heaven
Was fulfilled March 06, 2010.

Contents

Acknowledgments ix

1   Apologetic for the attractiveness of Jesus Christ 1
       (I Pet 2: 21–25)

2   Jacob's Ladder: Encountering God   14
       (Gen 28:10–22)

3   A Blank Check: Prayer Requests 25
       (I Kings 3:3–15)

4   Courtesy: No Trivial Pursuit 35
       (I Cor 13:4–8)

5   Faith or Faithfulness 42
       (Acts 6:1–6; Gal 5:22–23)

6   The Polluted Well 50
       (I Pet 2:1–3)

7   Reach the End, not the Top 57
       (Phil 3:12–16)

8   Jeremy's Egg 65
       (I Cor 15:12–19)

9   A New Heaven and New Earth 71
       (Rev 21:1–22:6)

10 In Loving Memory of My Beloved Mother 90

Acknowledgments

A LMOST IMMEDIATELY after the publication of *A Faith Worth Believing, Living and Commending*, many have requested me to publish another one of the same nature, with the populace as the target. As a sequel to that book, this book *Giving Wings to the Soul* is a collection of apologetic sermon, speeches or talks, exegetical and theological reflections, pastoral and devotional materials, most of them were delivered in notable occasions or events. The compilation began after the demise of my beloved mother, Madam Ngu Poh Teh, to whom this book is dedicated in loving memory of her. This was completed while at Wycliffe Hall, Oxford University, where I am appointed as Visiting Scholar, and I am indebted to Dr. Richard Turnbull, the principal of Wycliffe Hall, for his generous arrangement.

Special thanks must be extended to Dr. Anthony Cross, Regent's Park College, Oxford University, and Dr. Ravi Zacharias, whom my Centre honored as "the prince of apologists", for their generous commendations; and Dr. Matthew Knell, the Visiting lecturer at London School of Theology in England for his editorial task, which helps rescue me from innumerable lapses in style and frequent use of complex theological jargon. Any weakness in the book I shall not impute to them, but to myself, who is learning how to write in a way that gives wings to the soul.

Last but not least, I owe much to my Ceceilia for her continual support and quiet affirmation of my works in scholarship and service, and our son Hansel-Timon, whose hilarious humor and cheerful disposition has added to his parent joy upon joy. To God Be the Glory!

Dennis Ngien, PhD
Professor of Systematic Theology,
Tyndale Seminary, Toronto, Canada;
Founder, Centre for Mentorship & Theological Reflection,
Toronto, Canada
September 06, 2010

1

Apologetic for the attractiveness of Jesus Christ

(I Pet 2:21–25)[1]

R ICHARD HALVERSON, the former chaplain of the American senate, said that it is very easy for one to lose touch with the 'main thing.' And the main thing of the Christian life is a person, Jesus of Nazareth. Christianity began on Palestinian soil, Halverson continued, as a relationship with a person. When it moved to Greek soil, it became a philosophy. It then moved to Roman soil, and it became an institution; when it arrived on British soil, it became a culture; when it moved to America, it became an enterprise. However when it came to Canadian soil, what did Christianity become? It became new principles to live by, or anything that substitutes for the centrality of Jesus

1. This sermon was preached at the *Centre for Mentorship & Theological Reflection* 12th anniversary, June 10, 2010, held at Van Norman Worship & Study Centre at Tyndale University College & Seminary, Toronto. It was at this event where Dr. Ravi Zacharias was honored by the Centre as "the prince of apologists," in recognition of his worldwide contributions to the fields of apologetics and evangelism; and Nelly Chau was honored as the Centre's "Lay-leader" award recipient, in recognition of her long-term dedication and fervent service.

Christ, whose communion with his Father we participate in through the efficacy of the Holy Spirit.

Christianity is fundamentally about a relationship with a person—in loving, trusting, obeying, and worshipping. That is the 'main thing.' Therefore, the crucial task of an apologist or theologian is to keep the main thing as the main thing—the person of Christ—what he does or means to us, how he relates to us, and allow that to shine.

More than defending Christianity, apologetics is about commending the attractiveness of Jesus Christ, whose very attractiveness is to be found in the acts he performed for us. As a theologian, let me offer you a sample of these acts:

In I Pet 2:21–25, Peter identifies a three-fold misery of humanity: firstly, there is the misery of suffering and pain; secondly, the misery of guilt and sin; and thirdly, the misery of human straying and wandering. Indeed, we do suffer, we sin and we stray—the three-fold misery. And to each, Peter offered three Christological responses. He explained what Christ means, what he does or how he relates to us in the contexts in which we find ourselves.

First, when suffering comes, who is Christ for me? Peter wrote in verse 21: "Christ suffered for you." When we experience suffering and pain in our life's journey, we ask the questions: what does Christ mean to us now? What has he done? Where is God now? Does he really care? Is he distant, aloof or unconcerned?! Not at all! Peter simply responded: "Christ suffered for us." He is there in your pain. Peter wanted the wounded to perceive in the Cross God's deepest pain and his loving scars. Our names are written on the wounds of Christ, and he cares for us. "Contemplate the wounds of Christ," St. Augustine advised. Ponder them and our hearts shall be satisfied. When we do this, faith in Christ becomes a reasonable act and the most attractive thing.

When Philip asked, "show me the Father so that my troubled heart will be satisfied," Jesus replied: "He who has seen me has seen the Father" (John 14:9–10). Our conception of God is to be governed by Christ, not by human philosophy. Dorothy Sayers put this beautifully: "In Jesus Christ, God wrote his autobiography." For God is Christ-like, and in him is no un-Christ-likeness at all. As John Austin Baker says, "The crucified Jesus is the only accurate picture of God the world has ever seen." The sight of Jesus on the cross discloses God as one who suffers with humanity.

If we take the Trinity and the incarnation seriously and recognize that this human Jesus is the second divine person, we can say there is no suffering closer to God than the suffering of the human Jesus. Thus, the human suffering of Jesus is really God's own suffering: God suffers as we do; God suffers *humanly*, and he knows human pain first-hand. In the cross, there is no surrogate; no delegate; no representative; but God himself. "In Christ, God wrote his autobiography."

Christ is the sign and the substance of God's pure and boundless love. Christ is the mirror of the fatherly heart of the God who is at the center of the universe. True recognition of God is to be found in the crucified Christ, who led us to the Father in order that we might be seized by "the divine and kind paternal heart," one and the same heart—Christ's heart and the fatherly heart are identical—the perfect heart that beats with earnestness for us from eternity.

What is a Perfect Heart? A perfect heart is a broken heart: if your heart is never broken, it is imperfect and defective. The love by which Christ loves us is identical to his Father's love, the one and same love, which burns passionately for his creatures. Concretely we see the sign and substance of God's love in the suffering of the Cross, encapsulated in the words of St. Peter: "Christ suffered for you." He meets you where you are—in your pain where God is to be found. There your hearts will be satisfied, and you will be filled with a reciprocal love for him.

However, when speaking of God's suffering, a distinction must be made between suffering that defines God, and the suffering that describes God. Suffering is not that which God is, but that which he assumes. God does not suffer on account of his being as such, but on account of the act that he has performed in relation to us. Suffering is not an ontological predicate, not intrinsic to God's being, but is that which God undergoes or takes on as he enters into the plight of human condition.

Love is the essence of God, not suffering; suffering is a function of the love that is God's being. Yet love is not primarily God's being; it is primarily God's way of being. And there are two levels to this.

(i) Love is God's way of being in and for himself. In God's own life, love interpenetrates trinitarianly, supremely, and perfectly. There is a dynamism of love flowing and flaming through the Trinity. There is in God a perfect communion of love, and thus we may say that love is God's way of being in himself and for himself. While this is true, it is yet incomplete, for how God is in himself and for himself is precisely for himself, not yet for us. St. Bernard of Clairvaux asked: "What good is God if he is not God for me?" Bernard never wearied of repeating the two sweet words *pro me* (for me). (ii) The most dynamic assertion of the Christian faith is this: love is God's way of being for us (*pro nobis*), which is the essence of the Gospel. Precisely, the love manifested in Christ's suffering is God's way of being himself for us. It is in God's suffering for me where God is most himself: he is most divine or most Godlike not in majesty, but in humility; not in pomposity, but in suffering. God does not suffer out of any deficiency of being, but simply because he wills to love, to be my lover.

An impassable (non-suffering) deity does not care, and thus has no friends. St. Theresa of Avila complained: "God, you would have more friends if you had treated the ones you have a little better." An impassable God attracts no friends, and is thus a lonely God. But in contrast, the suffering God attracts friendship and incites worship. What converted me from Buddhism to Christianity was the Crucified Christ, whose heart is a burning love, a "glowing oven," flaming with love for me!

Michael Green, a seasoned evangelist whom I met recently at the *Oxford Centre for Christian Apologetics*, exhorted me in his beautiful British accent: "Dennis, the one thing the world needs to hear, and which we must tell is this: God loves you, whoever you are; and whatever class, color, creed, and country there is, God loves you." With deep conviction, Michael put his right hand on my forehead and repeated forcefully St. Peter's words: "Christ suffered," meaning "God suffered for the wounded; believe it with all your heart; proclaim it with all of your strength"—the glad tidings that has lifted the hearts of the countless wounded. How marvelous it is, in the presence of pain and loss, to be touched by the omnipotent love that suffers, and the perfect heart that is wounded for us!

Secondly, in the misery of sin, what does Christ mean? Peter believed that there is a savior who meets our needs: in verse 24, "he bore our sin in his body."

"Sin," Keith Miller wrote, "is the *Ultimate Deadly Addiction.*" It is a basic and all-consuming self-centeredness; a need to control in order to get what we want. It is a universal addiction to self that develops when one puts himself at the center of his personal world in a way that leads him to abuse others. It is self-absorption; it is an infection, a deadly infection. It is real, and each one of us is under its control to one degree or another. The only hostages in the world are not those that had been secreted away by tyrannical figures. We are all hostages to our selves, to what Malcolm Muggeridge called "the dark little dungeon of our ego." Sin is that deep-seated need to be our own Lord, leading to alienation from God and from each other, and resulting in bondage to drives and desires beneath our dignity, all of which culminates in death.

The chief symptom of sin is denial. Miller wrote: "Denial is the chief characteristic of sin as it is for traditional addiction." Neither sinners nor addicts can see the extent to which their addiction is ruining their own lives and relationships. This makes chronic addicts and self-absorbed sinners difficult to treat. Both are unaware of the disastrous effects that the disease has on them. Religious sinners and moralists are the hardest ones to treat, for they are adept at devising all kinds of ways of practicing denial. Is not the church's reluctance to use the word 'sin' an obvious proof of denial? We use all kinds of euphemisms for sin, like mistakes, lapses, ignorance, oversights, struggles or dysfunctions. No wonder we never know the joys of the gospel.

There is no natural knowledge of sin. The knowledge of what sin is has to be revealed by God, and thus is a predicate of God's grace. If we think that we can uncover sin by watching a few horror movies, we are simply too shallow and have not understood the human heart. The knowledge of sin does not flow from any creaturely beings, but from Jesus Christ. The cross drives its nails into our conscience in order to expose us to the horror of our systematic sinning. No apologetic artistry, theological edifice, psychological introspection, or any creaturely means is able to penetrate the human heart and disclose the magnitude of sin. "The heart is wicked and deceitful above all things—who can penetrate it?"

We are so blinded to our sinful nature by our sin that we require nothing less than the forsakenness of God in his Son's dereliction to expose it. No one can know the horror of sin unless the cross reveals it. The cross does not lie or trifle with us; it removes the masks of sin and names it as the sin it is. The cry—"My God, My God, Why hast thou forsaken me?"—is the revelation of our sin for which Christ suffered and died. It cost God greater pain to expose us to the horror of sin than it costs us when we become aware of it.

However dreadful we might feel at the knowledge of our sinfulness, we are never as heartbroken as God is himself. This knowledge frightened God's "only and dearest Son" so horribly that, in his final cry of misery on the cross, he experienced greater anguish than any human person has ever undergone. The severity of God's wrath was reflected most acutely in the cost that was required to appease it. It cost the loss of "God's very own Son," "the dearest child" (as Luther put it), who willingly offered to bear in pain the judgment for sin because of his compassion for us.

The horror of sin had to be exposed; the terror of God's wrath had to be appeased. The cross caused sin to appear, not that sin might forever remain in our conscience, in which case we would face sheer despair, but that sin might disappear from our conscience. Christ exposed our systemic evil within in order that he might dispose of it. He achieves this because he does what he does in his capacity as our sin-bearer. This is Peter's *pronouncement*, not just an *announcement*, but a pronouncement, declaring with absolute efficacy: "He bore your sins in his body." This means that Christ came to:

(a) take up our sin as his own,

(b) carry it in his body, and

(c) carry it off.

He bore the human infection of sin into the oblivion of nothingness. As a physician, Christ exposes you to the horror of your deadly infection while at the same time disclosing himself to you as the remedy for it. Pascal said: "Knowing God without knowing one's misery leads to pride; knowing our misery without knowing the redeemer leads to despair." Christ names the problem of your misery; correspondingly, he shows that he himself is the cure for it. This is God's way of being himself for us, by bearing our sin and suffering our judgment on the cross. Is that not the "main thing", the Gospel? John Calvin put this well: "when the Gospel was preached, the blood of Jesus Christ flows." And it does; it drips, and our hearts are sprinkled afresh.

The One God effects our atonement for us, and both the Father and the Son suffer, but in different ways: the Son suffered abandonment by his Father, who laid upon him the iniquities of us all; conversely, the Father suffered through forsaking/abandoning his Son, who bore the sin of the world. This relational separation/break that occurs between the Father and Son, which both the Father and the Son suffer from in different ways, is God's story with us. There is no essential/ontological separation, for God is indivisibly One in essence, without partition.

God does not love the world because it is *so big* that it takes the greatest kind of love to embrace it and to redeem it, but because the world is *so bad* that it takes the greatest kind of love to embrace it and to redeem it. The greatest love is God's self-giving love as revealed in the cross. As Darlene Zschech, a hymn writer romantically put it: "The Darling of Heaven" was crucified for us, by whose crucifixion we too become the Darling of Heaven. The distance between God and us, which was created by sin, is abolished. The purpose of God in saving us is not that we might be good, but that we might be HIS—the Darling of Heaven.

Through Christ's triumphant act on the cross, "we might die to sin, and live for righteousness", wrote Peter. Is that perfectionism? Not so. Is it triumphalism? Not at all. Rather it is an optimism of grace. Although we struggle with sin, it ceases to exist as "an inner necessity". While sin does remain in the Christian life, it has ceased to reign in it; sin continues to reside, but never presides; sin avails, but never prevails; instead, righteousness prevails. Christ presides and reigns; he prevails.

While we have no "inherent power" to conquer sin, we do have the "adherent power" to achieve this through our attachment to Christ, whose conquering power is granted to the adherents so that we might live in and under his kingdom, and serve him in everlasting righteousness, innocence, and blessedness.

Thirdly, in the misery of straying or wandering, how does Christ relate to us? Peter writes in verse 25: "You were like sheep gone astray, but now have returned to the shepherd and guardian of our souls." There is a double emphasis here: shepherd [guidance] and guardian [protection] are interchangeably one concept.

Mother Teresa of Calcutta was asked of which image of Jesus Christ in the Bible she preferred. Promptly she replied: "Jesus Christ as My Shepherd." Why? "Because life is a risky and dangerous business, and I need Christ to guide and protect." We are often like sheep. Sheep are primarily stupid, prone to wander and stray from their shepherds, as we do from the God whom we love. I need his guidance and his guardianship. Yes, I may stray, but there is the Shepherd; I may fall, but I will never fall out of or beneath his hands.

If you were to ask a Jew, "in what way is Jehovah real to you?" he will tell you a personal story, testifying to God's intimate involvement in his life. Testimony constitutes not a rational defense of faith, but a way of commending the relevance and attractiveness of faith in Jesus Christ. Testimony is intended not so much to convince people rationally, but to invite them to discern the signs of divine transcendence in people's lives, which might subsequently move them to apprehend, or rather be apprehended by, the beauty of Jesus Christ.

Let me share with you a story of how Christ is real to me, a personal testimony. Over 20 years ago, I was speaking to a group of university students. After the meeting, a person named Brian phoned me and insisted that I come to visit him in his house. I dropped by MacDonald, picking up two hamburgers and two cups of coffee. I intended to spend some time with Brian. Upon arriving, I discovered that the living room was dark and the whole house was smelly. Obviously he was on drugs and alcohol.

I called out, "Brian, I am here now. Turn on the lights so that I could see your face." He did. To my utter shock, he was holding a gun. My heart was pounding fast, my hands grew quickly cold and sweat began pouring down my face. He grinned at me as he pointed his gun at my forehead.

He said, "Tonight I wanted to die with you. I do not want to die alone. I've picked you to die with."

I asked fearfully, "Why me? Of so many preachers, why did not you select me? Why not Billy Graham, the prince of evangelists? Why not Ravi Zacharias, an Indian evangelist? Why a little guy like me, a Malaysian Chinese?" Then I heard a gunshot; a bullet went past my left ear.

He cried: "Tonight, I am going to kill myself, kill you, and kill everybody. The whole world stinks." Did you notice the order—kill myself, kill you, and kill everybody? With terror, I responded, "If you really want to do it in that order, then just do it."

He then regained his balance and said, "There are two reasons why I choose you to be my death-partner:

(i) I came from a broken family. I felt that you are the only one who truly understood my pain, and the messages you gave brought comfort to my heart.

(ii) I am confused," I replied, "If my messages brought you comfort, why do you still want to commit suicide? Why do you want to die with me?"

He said, "I wanted to die with you because you preached about love and heaven. You know the way to heaven, and you will go to heaven when you die. That is why I wanted to die with you, so that you could take me with you into heaven together." Of course, he was not thinking correctly, for he had been without food for days.

I said, "Brian, since we are going to die tonight, may I suggest that we have our last supper together. Here are two cups of coffees and two hamburgers. I wanted to know more about you; tell me your story so that I can die in peace."

6 1/2 hours I spent under the threat of a gun, and anything could happen. 6 1/2 hours of listening and praying as I engaged with Brian. I said, "I know life doesn't seem fair to you; it does not make sense. I don't know what God is doing in your life. Brian, if you cannot trust God's hands, would you open your heart and let God love you? Let Christ enter into your life to be your guide and guardian." And he did, after much pleading.

Today he is fully well physically, psychologically and spiritually. I believe that God was there, working out his salvation in a personal way.

Why am I narrating this? Is it to brag about how strong my faith is? No—I was scared to death. I do not have a strong faith that can move mountains. *My faith is weak and crummy, but God loves it when our faith is weak and crummy* because his strength is made perfect in our weakness. From this experience, I now know what Job meant when he said: "I have heard you with my ears, now I have seen you." I have come to a deeper realization, that life can indeed be risky and dangerous. But we have "returned," St.

Peter said, "to Jesus Christ, the shepherd and guardian of our souls." And Christ alone suffices to meet every need.

"Savior like a shepherd, lead us; much we need thy tender-care . . . we are thine; do thou befriend us; be the guardian of our way; keep thy flock from sin, defend us; seek us when we go astray."

For me, Christ is real. I must commend to you my Christ, who is real in my pain, in my struggle with sin, and in my daily walk with him. And the bonus is that Christ can also be real to you, if you will only open your heart to him and let him love you.

2

Jacob's ladder: Encountering God[1]

(Gen 28:10–22)

WHEN I was a teenager, I happened to meet Mother
Theresa briefly. Looking straight into my eyes,
probably perceiving evil in me, she said solemnly: "Young
man, seek to be good and generous to others; seek not to be
great; only God himself is great." The encounter with her
was memorable, invigorating, and thrilling. I used to brag
that I was in touch with greatness.

But what would it be like to meet God who is himself
Great? Mother Theresa was great, yet her greatness was not
essential, but causal; it was not inherent, but received. God
is great, but not by a greatness that he receives from others;
rather it is a greatness that he himself is. What would it be

1. This sermon was preached June 10, 2009, at the Centre for
Mentorship & Theological Reflection's 11th anniversary held at Van
Norman Study and Worship Center, Tyndale University College
and Seminary, Toronto, Ontario, Canada. It was at this event where
Professor Dr. Alister McGrath of Oxford Univeristy was honored as
the "Senior Scholar," in recognition of his outstanding contribution
to the fields of Historical and Systematic Theology, and Dr. Michael
Haykin of Southern Baptist Theological Seminary was the Preacher.

like to meet God, the Superlative Greatness, and to know that you have met him beyond any shadow of a doubt?

An anonymous wrote in his journal, "There is but one thing needful—to possess God, if only we could?" This is the basic question in life. How can I meet God? Where does God meet us? How can God cease to be a theoretical concept and become a living reality in my life? If we want to meet God personally, let us take a look at the ancient story of Jacob at Bethel. Let me summarize the story.

Crossing a dry, barren wilderness, Jacob came at night to a lonely place. There he lay down, using a stone from the hillside as a pillow. He dreamed about a ladder that was set up from earth to heaven, on which were ascending and descending the angels of God. Then he heard the voice of God. God came and renewed the covenant he had made with Jacob's forefathers, promising that his descendants would be a multitude and that all the families of the earth would be blessed through him. Jacob awoke from his sleep, and the vivid vision of God was still with him. He said to himself: "Surely the Lord was in this place, and I did not know it. How awesome is this place! This is none other than the house of God; the gate of heaven."

Now, what was the nature of the meeting place between God and Jacob? What kind of a place was Jacob in when God came alive to him? I have four Reflections on this:

IT WAS A PLACE OF QUIETNESS

Bethel is a place of rocky wilderness—bleak, dry, lonely, forbidding, and barren. It is also a place of craggy mountains and deep ravines. Jacob was there alone, quiet, under a starless sky. It was in the context of quietness that God encountered him.

To be clear, whenever we speak about meeting God, we must bear in mind that God cannot be stereotyped, and that he can meet us anywhere or in any way that he wills. God alone picks the place of divine-human encounter, not us. God is free to determine the conditions of his encounter with us. For instance:

For Isaiah, it was a temple where he saw the Lord high and lifted up;

For John, it was the forgotten island, where he saw the vision of the risen Christ;

For Luther, it was a tower where he had an evangelical breakthrough when he studied the book of Romans;

For Augustine, it was a garden, where he was made aware of his need for God;

For St. Francis of Assisi, it was a church as he knelt before a crucifix, and his soul was enflamed.

Therefore, there are endless varieties of religious experience, since God is never stereotypical, but always creative and redemptive. One condition that seems to prevail whenever we talk about meeting God is a place of solitude. There God's presence is most strongly felt. "Be still, and know that I am God."

Perhaps God is unreal to so many people because they are never still, or never quiet, and so they never hear the voice of God. They don't get to enjoy God because they don't get to be alone with God. They always live their lives against the background of noises and voices, haste and rush, pace and pressures; they never have time to wait for anything.

Do they want to meet God? Oh yes, but somehow life is too noisy and busy. No wonder God is so transcendent, so abstract and so impersonal to them.

Sisters and brothers, how can God be real to us if we never give him a quiet glade where we can rest with him?

Florence Allshorn, a distinguished Anglican woman, wrote:

> One thing I am very sure of is that for me just to wait *quietly* in the presence of God, doing nothing but fixing my mind on some expressive words—such as 'Oh God! Here I am; here you are. Father, my Father, Oh God! I want you. I want you with all my heart—makes a world of difference.' Just as lying under the sun, allowing the heat of the sun to blaze down on your body affects your body and senses, so waiting quietly in the presence of God affects your soul.

I firmly believe that, just as the sun changes the color of our body, so the transforming power of God changes us as we wait quietly in his presence. If you are quiet enough to let God speak to you, perhaps you might say as Jacob did: "Surely the Lord was in this place, and I did not know it."

IT WAS A PLACE OF HARDSHIP AND DISCIPLINE

Jacob had a very strange pillow. It was not soft, like the Dunlop pillow you slept on last night, but a stone picked from a craggy hillside, and on that he rested his head. This was very unusual for Jacob, because he was a lover of ease and comfort, a man of indulgence, an egotistical man.

There he was, without a companion and without a home, fully exposed to the danger of wild beasts, in a place of discipline and hardship, using a stone as a pillow. When he was reduced to his last necessity, the Lord came with a remarkable oracle, with a stream of assurances flowing from the centrality of God's being, the superabundant sweetness.

Isn't it true that great visions often come to a person when there is an element of hardship and discipline, even suffering? The philosopher Thomas Carlyle put this correctly: "All pure thoughts and all deep insights are the daughters of pain." He claimed that when men and women really discover something worthwhile, it is usually in a place of hardship and suffering. It is there where they are most creative, most perceptive and most dynamic. I am a living proof of this. When I was struggling with infirmity and inconveniences, three academic books were published within a short, difficult period. At that time I was most innovative and productive.

A champion athlete was once interviewed by a journalist. "Mr. Champion, you have strived to reach the top. Do you still get up early in the morning as you used to, jogging around the mountains and the fields while the dew is still on the ground?"

With honesty, he replied: "It becomes difficult for a man to get up so early when he starts wearing silk pajamas."

What is the champion saying? He is saying that, where there is an absence of hardship and suffering, you begin to lay back and you don't dream the dreams you once had, you no longer see the vision you used to. You are not at your most creative. Yes, it gets harder to know God when life is too easy and too smooth. When there is too much comfort and ease, we tend to become complacent, self-reliant and turned in upon ourselves.

Then come 'sorrows like sea billows,' and we begin to see that God is so vital and that we need him to see us through our hidden fears and hidden tears. In suffering we are thrown back at the foot of the cross, and we discover again the wonderful news: "God was there in my pain; he felt and knew it first-hand."

Many people have made important discoveries when they had a stone for a pillow. Suffering, a gift that nobody wants, may be consecrated as a place where people discover something worthwhile about God, life and themselves.

Helen Keller, blind and deaf from birth, a prolific author of 12 books and a well-known leader, has this to say: "I thank God for my handicaps, for through them, I have found myself, my worth and my God."

IT WAS A PLACE OF SELF-EXAMINATION/ SELF-DISCOVERY

Why was Jacob crossing the wilderness? Why was he sleeping beneath the open sky with a stone for a pillow? Well, he was a fugitive. He was a scoundrel, a cheater; he cheated his brother Esau out of his birthright. Esau, a hot-blooded man, swore that he would kill him. So Jacob had to flee as fast as he could to another land, sleeping with a hard stone for a pillow, in this place of quietness and hardship; and thus Bethel became a place of self-examination, where Jacob became acquainted with himself, and came face-to-face with God.

A young fellow told his girlfriend, "Last night I dreamed that I was proposing to you. I wonder what that means." The girl said: "That is simple. That means you have more sense when you are asleep than when you are awake." It is not a delusion when God operates in the mind of the Patriarch, but a revelation. God hides in a dream in order to reveal, and as a result Jacob came to his senses. He learned about himself, as intimated by Calvin, that he was at variance with God; but he also learnt about God, that God was not adverse to him.

One reason why people today don't meet God is because they are too shallow, too superficial; they are always posing and pretending; pretending to be an intellectual elite; more concerned about status-seeking, about their own pleasure and about comfort than they are about their spiritual lives. They hardly ever confront themselves in any depth. They don't ask the big questions of life: Who am I? Why am I still alive? What about my sins and wrongdoings? They hardly ever come to a place of self-examination. Yet they are fully occupied in the business of examining others, pointing fingers at others and finding faults in others. They skate over the surface of life; they never go too deep, so they never meet God in any depth.

C. S. Lewis, on the eve of his conversion, immersed himself in self-examination. "For the first time in my life, I examined myself with a seriously practical purpose, and what I discovered horrified me: A zoo of lusts; a bedlam of ambitions, a nursery of fears, a harem of fondled hatreds. My name is Legion." It was in self-acquaintance that Lewis discovered God. He met God as a God of mercy, a God who claimed Lewis for himself. Like Jacob in a place of darkness of mind and perversity of heart, he too would say: "Surely the Lord was in this place."

Catherine of Siena, the medieval theologian, had several visions of God. When plunged in the depths of filth and darkness, at the place of self-discovery, she cried out: "Oh God, where were you where I was in filth and darkness?"

"My daughter, where was I? I was in your heart," said Lord.

BETHEL IS A PLACE OF SURPRISE—BY PURE AND BOUNDLESS GRACE

Grace always *surprises* us where we *least expect* it, but when we *most need* it. Jacob did not expect God to come at all; he was no returning prodigal, he was not looking for God. Yet there came the ladder, and Grace descended to entreat him, without a word of rebuke or demand. The Grace that descended upon Jacob was that by which he ascended to heaven. Jacob did not climb the ladder, did not espouse a spirituality of human effort in which he measured which rung of the ladder he had reached.

Theologically, the ladder is Jesus Christ himself (cf. John 1:51), the one who connects heaven and earth; the mediator who ministers the things of God to us and takes our things to him. The Grace that flows from the Father through the Son is that by which we rise to the Father through the Son. Luther said: "Apply ourselves to Jesus' humanity, Jacob's ladder, from there we ascend to the divinity."

It is all Grace that breaks into Jacob's life, seizes him, and in the end transforms the scoundrel into the prince of God. It is Grace that (a) breaks in, (b) breaks down every hindrance to access to God, causing Jacob to finally (c) break out in reverential fear: "How awesome is this place, for this is none other than the house of God!" It is Amazing Grace that taught my heart to fear, and grace my fears relieved. Not only does Grace excite us, it also inspires in us fear and pious submission. Grace is the causative agency of our reverential worship.

Jacob's experience of God is indeed a surprising, stunning, and startling display of God's Grace. Precisely because of his unworthiness and sinfulness, the opposite of righteousness and goodness, Jacob proves himself to be the person whom God loves. Luther put it so beautifully: "Sinners are lovely because they are loved by God: they are not loved because they are lovely."

It was Pure Grace, descending upon him in order to raise him up. Did you notice how relevant God's grace was for Jacob, that every promise God made met Jacob's needs?

Here he was, away from home, a mommy's boy, lonely, and feeling god-forsaken. God said: "I am with you."

Fearing that Esau might kill him, God said: "I will keep you."

Not knowing what hardship he might have to face, God said: "I promise safe return."

Uncertain of his future, God sealed in his heart his invincible promise: "I will not leave you until I have done what I have promised" (verses 15–16).

Is there anything more wonderful than this? Thus, in addition to Rick Warren's emphasis on the "Purpose-Driven Church", I propose the "Promise-Driven Church", standing on the promises of God. God's promise never becomes God's prison. God who is free in making the promise remains free in fulfilling it. Thus we can confidently hope for the fulfillment of his promises. The promises (a) emanate from God, (b) point us to God, and finally (c) drive us to God. But *which God?* The silent God? No, the "never-speechless" God, the ever-speaking God, whose voice is a sweet sound in our ears: "I am your God" [So generous was his claim]; and by that efficacious voice, our identity as God's beloved is (a) constituted, (b) confirmed, and (c) cemented. "I am His" [So efficacious is the causality of his Word].

CONCLUSION

The God with whom we have to do is the God of Abraham, Isaac, and now Jacob, three succeeding generations and many more; for God spans the generation gap. No one can domesticate God or confine him to the past. God is the same yesterday, today, and forever. His grace is inexhaustible, forever sufficient, if only we believe.

An artist painted a picture of Niagara Falls, that marvelous beauty that has attracted tourists from all over the world. The picture was well-painted and no one had any difficulty in identifying what it was—it was Niagara Falls. The painting was to be hung in an exhibition. The night before the exhibition, they discovered that the artist had not given the painting a name. The artist has already left town, but they did not want simply to leave it that way. Eventually one person came up with a perceptive title. Gazing at the water pouring down the Niagara Falls, he put these words at the bottom: "More to Follow."

What he was saying is this: for all these years and centuries, millions of tons of water have poured over these cataracts, and still "there is more to follow, more to descend, more to be poured down." That is the Gospel. It invites us to come to God, a place of unlimited supply, from whom believers down through every generation have drawn tremendous resources and help. And yet there is always more to follow, more to come. The grace that descends from the Father through the Son in the Holy Spirit is totally adequate to meet our needs.

> O for a thousand tongues to sing;
> My great Redeemer's praise;
> The glories of my God and king;
> The triumphs of His Grace!

3

A Blank Check

Prayer Requests

(I Kings 3:3–15)[1]

I N I Kings 3:5–15, we read about Solomon's dream. In that dream, God came to him and said, "Ask for whatever you want me to give" (verse 5). In other words, God was saying: "Solomon, I am going to give you a blank check. Fill in whatever you want. Ask, and it shall be done." Confronted with a new situation, in which he was made king in place of his father David, Solomon filled this into his check: "O Lord, grant me a wise and discerning heart so that I know how to govern" (verse 9). And it was granted him, and he was made the wisest of all in the East.

Professor Reinhold Niebhur was a great American theologian at Harvard University. The president of Harvard

1. This sermon was preached June 05, 2008, at the Centre's 10th anniversary, during which Dr. Timothy George was honored as the "Senior Scholar," in recognition of his outstanding contribution to the fields of historical theology and ecclesial piety, and Dr. Victor Shepherd as the "Best Preacher", in recognition of his homiletical gift and theological depths. Dr. Michael Haykin of Southern Baptist Theological Seminary gave a tribute to Dr. George, and Dr. Kevin Livingston of Tyndale Seminary gave a tribute to Dr. Shepherd.

University so highly esteemed his brilliance and character that he promised to give Professor Niebhur any chair or position, if only he chose to accept it. Many years ago, though not in an identical context as in Solomon, Professor Niebhur filled in a blank check, with three prayer requests:

> God, grant me grace to accept with serenity the things I cannot change;
> the courage to change the things I can;
> and the wisdom to know the difference.

With some variations, this beautiful prayer forms the background of my reflection tonight.

THE SERENITY TO ACCEPT THE THINGS I CANNOT CHANGE

Serenity means calmness of heart. It means accepting life as it comes to us, not grudgingly, but graciously; not with hostility, but with tranquility of mind.

We can all make a list of things over which we have no control, and that we cannot change. For instance, we cannot change the date and place of our birth; nor can we change our parental heritage. You cannot change your height, although you can change your weight.

What about bereavement—the loss of a near and dear one, or a physical or incurable sickness? What about unrealized dreams such as the catastrophes that occurred in China and Burma, over which no one had any control? You could look at these events, storm into heaven, and shout: "life is not fair." In fact, it isn't. You could look at the collapsed debris that covered the dead bodies or gaze at the lively primary school, which had once been filled with the noises and voices of little children, but now became the burial site of those lovely faces—the horrible and unbearable sight—and be totally cast down. You may look at those who suffer with open wounds that nothing could heal save the heavenly touch, and complain that life does not make sense. Indeed, it does not. You could sit and complain all day long until you lose your sanity and your balance. But that would not help you, would it?

When sorrows like sea billows rise, you have a choice: you can either lock yourself up in utter despair; or you can face them and accept the situation with a serenity that only God can supply. Ask for peaceful calm and it shall be given to us if only we believe. Fill it in that blank check with: "Oh Lord, grant me grace to accept with serenity the things about which I have no control, and things I cannot change." And the heavenly serenity that surpasses all understanding will flood into our feeble hearts.

What about the inequality of gifts? This ecumenical audience makes evident the unequal distribution of gifts. A doctrine of equality is an absolute absurdity. Yes, we are created equal in worth and dignity in the sight of God; but we are manifestly unequal in our natural endowments. We do not possess equal power, wealth, or health; we do not have the same opportunities. Gifts or blessings differ between individuals. One person has brain power to spare, another is intellectually mediocre; one person is a sparkling beauty, while another is just the opposite; one hardly has a day of illness in his life, abounding in good health for years and years, and is thus able to achieve much, while another hardly manages a day without pain and sickness, and is thus incapacitated. These inequalities are part of life. It is on these terms that life is given to us.

We should not look at the inequality of gifts with envy, as a green-eyed monster, but through the principle of stewardship; we are not the absolute owners of anything, but the responsible stewards of everything. One day we must give an account for all this. If I were a man with one talent, I ought not to stay up late, tossing and turning with envy because I have not got two talents or five talents. I should not sulk in resentful obscurity because I am made this way. Such invidious comparison has caused many miseries and disharmony in the church. We are called to be faithful with what we have, not with what we lack. And so there is no need for comparison or competition.

I am not trying to be a better preacher than Dr. Victor Shepherd, but I am trying to be a better preacher than I was last week. I am not trying to be a better writer and speaker than Dr. Timothy George, but I am trying to do better than last year. Thus I am able to rejoice in their greater gifts or opportunities, and make them my own by celebrating their efforts and celebrating with them. One of the greatest benefits of the communion of the saints is the communion of gifts for mutual edification.

The measure of stewardship is not success, but faithfulness; not popularity, but obedience; not being better than others, but humbly serving all; not reaching the top, but reaching the end; not glory, but suffering. And only a heart full of tranquility can embrace these radical reversals, which are diametrically opposed to the world's standards. This is what it means, using Luther's term, to be a theologian of the cross: to embrace the radical reversal; not glory, but suffering service.

In 2004, I was very ill. A few people wrongly heard that I had passed on to glory. So, sadly, they exchanged emails about my death, until they were corrected. One of these emails was forwarded to me, and it was a tribute to the deceased: "The late Dr. Dennis Ngien was no ivory-towered theologian; no Ivy League scholar. He was not well-known in Public Academia, but privately he was invaluable in small parts. The [coffin—misspelt word] coffee drinker with pastors and students; the table-talker with scholars and thinkers; the skilful encourager . . . this hidden secret is a treat and a treatment, but in small and memorable ways." What a wonderful tribute—a generous compliment, but also a demanding challenge!

This might become an epitaph or an obituary notice upon my future death. When I read it, I was amused by it, not offended by it. Is that how you think of me? If so, I thank you wholeheartedly for your affirmation of my gifts and my personality. Yes, I am no great theologian in the public academia; but I thank God that he has allowed me to play small parts in his Kingdom in enabling others to fulfill themselves and to actualize their callings as well as I can. I am no Ivy League scholar, which I accept with serenity. Praise God for those who precede me and exceed me. Each one of us, whether we are one-talented or ten-talented, can receive the same commendation from our Lord Jesus: "Well-done, thou good and faithful steward." Christ's commendation is a sweet sound in our ears. It is also the dynamic of a serenity that the world can neither offer nor understand.

THE COURAGE
TO CHANGE THE THINGS I CAN

Most of us find it hard to cope with change. In fact, we resent it. In an interview with an 82-year old man, a writer inquired: "Mr. You are now 82. You must have gone through numerous changes in your long life." The old man replied: "Yes, too many changes, and I am against every one of them." "Why?" "Because it is too upsetting and painful to change; it is too inconvenient, and too frightening to change." He eventually became a very miserable old man, precisely because of a lack of courage to face changes.

May I say this: one of the wishes of any dying ministry or organization is to refuse to change, to say that we have never done it this way before, so we are not going to try it now. When this Centre's ministry was born in 1998, many said that it could not be done. This Centre is:

(a) not a building, but a name;

(b) not a facility, but a fellowship;

(c) not a school, but a vision;

(d) not an institution, but a ministry.

In fact, many looked at it with suspicion and skepticism. Mockingly, they said: "Can anything good come out of this?" Some even chastised me: "Dennis, you were a crusader for 10 years. I cannot see you moving from preaching to 20,000 people to mentoring 1–2 persons, changing from the public arena to the private sphere. That is not you. It does not fit your personality or our expectations. It is an isolated, lonely ministry. You won't last. After all, it would be a waste of talent! One day, people will no longer hear of you; you will have become obsolete."

Yet God has a sense of humor! For ten years, I took risks and had a few setbacks; but I never lacked and have no regrets. I did what God enabled me to do, and will continue until further notice from above.

Paul Tillich, with whose theology I generally disagree, had this to say: "He who risks and fails can be forgiven; but he who never risks and therefore never fails is already a failure in the totality of his being." A courage to risk and to change is a by-product of our communion with a God who promises to go through these changes with us.

In the past 10 years, with a God-given courage, I have walked alongside pastors and leaders to assist them to:

(a) overcome their fear of the new, the uncertain and the unknown;

(b) fight complacency and insecurity;

(c) conquer fatalism and negativism; and

(d) foster order and discipline.

At the end of our journeys, both the mentor and mentorees have together increased their knowledge of God and themselves.

Perhaps one of the greatest victories in life is to possess a God-given courage to face myself—my own insecurity and my own systematic evil. By the grace of God, I can face these and conquer them.

THE WISDOM TO KNOW THE DIFFERENCE

Ten years ago, I took the liberty to change Niebhur's last prayer item to: "O Lord, grant me a joyous entrance into Wisdom-fullness, which thou art. Let me enjoy you daily." Notice that I use wisdom not adjectivally, but substantively. God is not great by a greatness that he receives from elsewhere, but by a greatness that he himself is. Likewise, God is not wise by a wisdom that he receives from others, but by virtue of who he essentially is—namely wisdom. It is not an adjectival genitive, that he has, but a subjective substantive, that he is. God is wisdom in his essence, just as he is love in his essence.

In 1998, my prayer was this: "Oh Lord, grant me a joyous entrance into Wisdom-fullness, which is God himself." In 2008, in an expanded fashion I pray: "O Lord, let me enjoy the abundant sweetness, which you are." The Westminster Shorter Catechism stated: "Man's chief end is to glorify God [and] enjoy him forever." Let me be audacious enough to render this differently: "Man's chief end is to glorify God by enjoying him forever." This concurs with Jonathan Edwards, who said: "When those who see God's glory delight in it, God is more glorified than if they only see it." This is the heart of worship: "God is most glorified when he is most enjoyed; most worshipped when he is most delighted."

However, there are impediments to our enjoyment of God's sweetness:

(i) The impulsive: those who are not reflective enough or thoughtful enough tend to be too hasty and sometimes nasty; they are generally superficial and hardly ever read.

The younger generation is intellectually sluggish, and in some extreme cases even intellectually retarded due to a lack of exercise of the mind. They are the action-oriented impulsive, mostly devoid of depth and content. Because reading is not their discipline and books are not their companions, their minds are not stretched. No wonder that many sermons are substantially shallow and theologically sloppy. May I say this: if you are a full-time pastor, your reading capacity ought to be at least 8 hours per week; otherwise, you are not fulfilling your role as a preacher-teacher. If you are a lay-leader, then your reading capacity ought to be at least 3 hours per week; otherwise, you will miss out on much of God's wisdom.

(ii) The compressive: those who tend to procrastinate, pile things up, and compress them into one time frame, and expect miracles to come of this. It isn't that these people don't know God's will; they may be very sensitive to God's guidance, but their problem is that they delay in acting out what God wants them to do. They fail to respond to the light that wisdom's fullness provides. They push things aside or leave them till later, and then they pick up more things along the way; thus they become so diversified in their interests that nothing is ultimately done or, if anything is done, it is done poorly. Bernard of Clairvaux, the only man whom Luther considered worthy of the name of "father" in faith, has this to advise: "not to progress is to regress, which is sin; to delay is sin." By delaying, the compressive makes no significant advances toward God, and thus fails to attain to wisdom's stability. Dear brothers and sisters, learn to walk within reach of God's revelation, and enjoy him as he comes to you.

Reading and writing are part of my spiritual journey with God. Each book that I have written was an occasion for enjoying God. I prayed as St. Anselm did: "O God, let me know and love You, so that I may rejoice in [enjoy] You." Enjoying God must not be done compressively, but progressively—step by step, with each passing moment, grasping the most of him, or rather being grasped by him so that his beauty may be formed in us. It takes time to enjoy God and to appropriate his gifts that are promised in the Son and communicated to us by the Holy Spirit. Every step I took, I gained a greater delight in him. My greatest discovery has been this: God cannot be outmaneuvred, only enjoyed—partially here, but fully there.

Dear friends, enter daily into the joy of the Lord, the Divine Superlative. Prostrate yourselves before the Wisdom-fullness and acknowledge as Solomon did: "I am but a little child" (verse 7). And this child-like humility is a condition of the possibility of an extravagant enjoyment of God's abundant sweetness.

Praise God for the past ten years. The hymn "All the Way My Savior Leads Me" rings true. Where will I be 10 years from now? I don't know, but I don't panic. I echo the words of Soren Kierkegaard: "Cram today with eternity, not with the next day." Cram today with eternity, and with God's abundant sweetness. Trust that the God who has led the way will continue to show the way.

4

Courtesy: No Trivial Pursuit

(I Cor 13:4–8)[1]

I Cor 13 has been the principal text of my daily devotions. Almost every day I read I Cor 13 to myself, Paul's marvelous hymn of praise to love. Great profit can be gained from a daily meditation on this chapter. In fact, I Cor 13 is the teleological principle of all that I do—in scholarship, preaching or any form of service. I aspire to pursue love in the most excellent way.

Carved into the philosophy department of an American university were these words: "Nestle into the mind of Plato, and think from there." That is what a philosopher does—thinks from the mind of Plato. Paul would paraphrase this slogan thus: "Nestle into the mind of Christ, and think from there." And this is what he did, for the prime subject of Paul's imagination when he wrote I Cor 13 was none other than Jesus Christ. Christ was the focus of Paul's contemplation when he wrote I Cor 13. Christ is patient, and so love is patient; Christ is kind, and so love is kind; Christ is not

1. This sermon was delivered at Tyndale Seminary's Commissioning Service for Chinese Graduates April 29, 2007, at Grace Chinese Gospel Church, North York, Ontario, Canada.

self-serving, and so it is with love; Christ is not arrogant, and so love is not arrogant; Christ is not rude, and so love is not rude. This last is the current focus of our reflections, verse 5: "Love is not rude." J. B. Philips paraphrased this beautifully. "Love has Good Manners." Love is always courteous, well mannered and polite. Jesus Christ, who was love incarnate, and graciousness embodied, was courteous towards the least, the last, and the lost. If you are serious about Christ, then good manners are no trivial pursuit.

In this commissioning service, let us think together about three areas where good manners and courtesy are very much required.

The first area is that of controversy and conflict. In our relationships with those who are opposed to us, those who disagree with us, good manners are very necessary.

To be sure, controversy and situations involving conflict are inevitable. If we have minds that can think and if we possess strong convictions, we are bound to enter into situations of conflict and disagreement. A lot of people don't like arguments. They try to stop or avoid all controversial arguments, fearing that they may create a bad atmosphere or generate enmity. Of course, if controversy is conducted with bad manners, if conflict is not handled with courtesy, they can become everything that we dislike, and everything that is contrary to the character of Christ.

What is the purpose of controversies or disagreements? The object of any controversy should be the discovery of truth. Controversy is a mental exercise. Through assessing different opinions, we are able to come to a clearer and deeper understanding of an issue. The object of arguments is not to make others look small or stupid, not to put others down or humiliate them; that indicates a lack of style. Rather, when a controversy is conducted with courtesy, it should be possible for people to differ and yet remain friends with each other.

Courtesy is demanded of us in the heat of an argument. Thus we may pause and say: "Christ is present here; let's do this in the spirit of Christ—with courtesy." John D. Rockefeller was a wealthy man, who had built the Riverside Baptist Church in New York. He was on the committee of the church, opposing a certain course of action that was being proposed. In a heated discussion, he spoke graciously against it, and voted against it. But when the majority carried out that course of action contrary to his advice, instead of resigning, Rockefeller assumed the chair of the committee that was set up to implement the decision that had been made. There was no name-calling or slandering. With courtesy and humility, he befriended those who were opposed to him. Despite conflicting convictions, he worked with his opponents within the same church to the end. Oh yes, J. D. Rockefeller was a man of intense zeal; but he was also a man of great courtesy.

Oh how I covet it—a combination of:

a) zeal and courtesy;

b) enthusiasm and good manners;

c) passion and politeness.

Secondly, we need courtesy in the area of proximity and equality, in our relations with those who are in closest proximity to us and those who are equal to us—our spouses. There is a need for spousal courtesy.

Beverley Nicol wrote a book entitled: *Are They the Same at Home?* This examines prominent people and their public lives. Beverley wonders speculatively how they are at home, around people who are near and dear to them? Are they as courteous to their spouses at home as they are in public? This is an acid test for all of us: are we the same at home as we are in public? Some people become so cynical that they regard "home as a place where you are tired of being nice to people." It is sad to say, but there is some truth to this. How many of us go home to our loved ones exhausted from work, having spent all day being nice to people in the office, church or faculty meeting. By the time we get home, we are exhausted, and our home becomes a place where we are tired of being nice, even to our loved ones, to those who are near and dear to us.

How can we be so accustomed to each other that we cease to be polite? It is said that familiarity breeds contempt. Not so, but familiarity does provide an occasion for discourtesy. We can take our spouses for granted. Precisely because of a lack of courtesy or consideration, homes can be turned into boxing rings, and romantic dinners can become courtrooms for prosecutions and harsh criticisms. Many couples stay up late at night when they should be sleeping. Why? Because of harsh and unkind words that have been flung against each other. In some extreme cases, people have to depend on tranquilizers in order to get to sleep. Allow me to say this: Courtesy is the best, most effective tranquilizer that could send your lover to sleep far quicker than any medication. Gentleness is the best aid to a good marriage— it oils the gears of life and makes living together both easier and sweeter. If you are serious about loving, then courtesy is a serious pursuit. What does it profit you if you gain popularity as a pastor or businessman, but lose your family?

When Winston Churchill was the Prime Minister of Great Britain, his marriage was considered to be one of the best examples. He was the epitome of loyalty and courtesy. Often when he gave a speech in the House of Commons, he would not begin until he had a sign from his beloved wife. Mutual respect and kindness were evident in their marriage.

Later in his life, someone interviewed Mr. Churchill and asked, "If you could live again, what would you want to be?" With a twinkle in his eyes, he replied, "Mrs. Churchill's next husband."

What a great benediction on marriage! And what a monumental compliment to his wife! And that is stylishness. Dear partners in the Gospel, be fervent in your service of God, but remember this: Proximity and Equality demand courtesy—including spousal courtesy.

Finally, courtesy is needed in the area of authority and power; in our relationships with those who are under us, we must conduct ourselves with good manners.

To be sure, authority in itself is not evil; it is in its abuse and misuse that it becomes evil. For the love of authority and power, some people work themselves and others into ill health, sacrificing pleasure and leisure. In the name of power, they will even sacrifice their manners. As a result, the church can become a stage on which to strut, or to express their vital complex. They forget that all authority is derived and entrusted, and must therefore be held and upheld in humility and with decency.

Company presidents, executives, and leaders are vested with authority and the power to rule and govern. But the fundamental purpose of conferring authority is enablement; when you are entrusted with authority, you are commissioned to enable those who are under you to soar and succeed.

5 years ago, a godly elderly pastor came to my office with his son, and I cannot forget the conversation we had. "Professor Ngien, you are a man of authority. This is my son John, and I now submit him to your authority and care, and place him under your tutelage. I believe good will come of this. Make my son a better servant." He understood the close connection between authority and the power that goes with it. Honestly, I struggled about whether or not to receive John—unpolished, unstructured, unfocused, arrogant, and full of himself. I almost dropped his name from the register. Then I remembered his father's words: "You are a man of authority; I am submitting my son to your care, hoping that you might enable John to soar and be a better servant." I almost lost my manners, were it not for I Cor 13:5—"Love has good manners." Praise God that John has become a faithful, humble pastor.

The church is filled with all sorts of people who are under your authority and care:

Some people are like wheels—they don't work unless they are pushed.

Some people are like trailers—they have to be pulled along.

Some people are like kites—always up in the air and, if you don't keep a hold on them, they fly away.

Some people are like canoes—they have to paddled.

Some people are like footballs—you never know which way they are going to bounce next.

Some people are like flat tires—they have to be jacked up.

Some people are like ice-cubes—they have to melted by your warmth.

Some people are like balloons—they are always puffed up, and you never know when they are going to blow up.

Some people are like good watches—pure gold, open faced, always on time, dependable, quietly busy and full of good works.

This rich variety of people is in the church and they are put under your authority, your direction and your care. As Charles Wesley's song proclaims, all of them have gained an interest in our Savior's blood. They are worth the precious blood of Jesus Christ. Love them all; be courteous to them. If you want to have a quarrel with the church, make sure that it is a lover's quarrel with the church. True love compels us to manifest good manners and courtesy. A rude Christian is a contradiction in terms. It is a bad advertisement for Tyndale University College and Seminary, and for our faith,

Peter Marshall, the former Chaplain to the American Senate, used to pray this for those who are in power and authority: "Oh God! When we are wrong, make us willing to change. When we are right, make us easy to live with." All of us are God's beloved people, so we should be a courteous people, polite in our manners and making it easier for people to come to us whatever the circumstances may face. Let us go out from here to whatever vocation we are called to and do something beautiful for Christ.

5

Faith or Faithfulness[1]

(Acts 6:1–6; Gal 5:22–23)

In Acts 6, a proposal was made that the church should select seven men to do the ministry of caring for widows. One of these was named Stephen, whom the Scripture described as: "a man full of faith or faithfulness [synonymous] and of the Holy Spirit" (Acts 6:5). Like Barnabas, Stephen was "a man of faith," because he was a man who was "full of the Holy Spirit." What a compliment!

The word faith or faithfulness means firmly and resolutely to stick to a person, to stay committed to a group, a cause or a belief without wavering. To be full of faith or faithful is to be constant, unwavering, loyal, and dependable.

May I say that this quality is in short supply, since so many people are yearning for popularity. Theodore Roosevelt proposed a contrary perspective: "It is better to be faithful than famous." Mother Teresa said: "I do not pray for success, I ask for faithfulness"—unwavering trust in God and a stubborn dedication to the task assigned by the

1. This sermon was preached February 14, 2009 in North Toronto Chinese Alliance Church, where I assisted Rev. Stephen Lam as Advisory Pastor of the English congregation for a year.

Master. St. Paul said that what is required of a servant is that he must be found faithful (I Cor 4:2).

Let me propose that we consider together three areas where faithfulness is needed.

Firstly, in the area of marriage and the family, faithfulness is an absolute necessity, without which marriages and families will disintegrate and collapse.

There is an intrinsic link between faithfulness and truthfulness. Rev 19:11, in speaking of the name for Jesus, brought these two together: His name is "faithfulness and truth." A faithful spouse is a truthful one—he is true in his vows, his words, and his promises. I ask myself: am I true to my wife? If I am true to her in my words and deeds, then I shall remain faithful, because you cannot have faithfulness without truthfulness. Nor can we have truthfulness without faithfulness. A truthful spouse is a faithful one; the marriage will last to the end. This is the character of Jesus, whose "faithfulness and truth" co-exist in his person perfectly. No wonder Marcus Cicero said, "nothing is more noble and more venerable than fidelity." He expands the word fidelity to include truth. "Faithfulness and truth are the most sacred excellences and endowments of the human mind."

We need faithfulness and truthfulness for our marriages to blossom, and to keep the original valentine love flaming and burning until the sunset hours.

I suggest one practical point, without oversimplification, that we may seek to follow: "to make up our mind before we make our bed every morning."

This is not achieved through romance, although we need this and are all better and stronger because of it, but it is resolution that keeps marriages together; and through resolution, we are able to conquer temptation. It is when we are double-minded, wavering in our minds, that we fall into temptation, and then bail out of a seemingly happy marriage.

However, with daily resolution we are able to shut the door to temptation; we will stay away from the lusts of the flesh. Without resolution, we will inevitably end up in a ditch from which there is no return. Resolution is to be made between a living room or the bedroom; between burning passion within the marriage or outside a marriage. There are people who are always looking for greener grasses. Do you not know that all green grasses will fade? As we age, we grow older with a fading beauty. Beauty is fleeting; but virtue is everlasting. In the times we live in, with an increasing number of marriages ending up in divorce, this particular quality of faithfulness is particularly needed. If God brings you a wonderful mate and wonderful children, then He expects you to be found loyal and faithful in your personal relationships with them.

Make a daily commitment to your spouse that he/she is your valentine love. Make up your mind to love your mate before you make up your bed. Strong commitments are not made at the wedding ceremony when the organ is playing, the romance is flowing, the flowers smell good, the people are beautiful and brilliant with their attractive gowns and attire, plus all the tears of joy, kisses and embraces—all of these help to adorn the wedding occasion. Rather, strong commitments are made daily—I make up my mind to stick with my wife before I make up my bed. Marriage does not end at the wedding ceremony, but begins there. It ought to be nourished and nurtured, not simply through romance but through daily resolution: I must make up my mind before I make up my bed.

I once read a resolution prayer of commitment to marriage, which I now recite frequently:

> I am standing for the healing of my marriage! I won't give up, give in, give out or give over till that healing takes place. I made my vow, I said the words, I gave the pledge, I gave a ring, I took a ring, I gave myself, I trusted God, and I said the words, and meant the words . . . in sickness and in health, in sorrow and in joy, for better or worse, for richer or poorer, in good times and in bad times, so I'm standing now, and won't sit down, let down, slow down, calm down, fall down, look down, or be down till the breakdown is torn down.
>
> In a world of filth, I'll stay pure; surrounded by lies, I will speak the truth; where hopelessness abounds, I'll hope in God; where revenge is easier, I'll bless instead of curse; and where the odds are stacked against me, I'll trust in God's faithfulness. I'll listen not to the prophet of gloom and doom. I'm a stander . . . I have made my choice, set my face, entered the race, believed the Word, and trusted God for all the outcomes. I will not blow up or give up until my marriage is healed up or built up.

Make up your mind daily before you make up your bed, and faithfulness may be assured.

Secondly, in the area of our service, faithfulness is necessary; without it we will surely quit or resign.

Most of us wrestle with God because we are very impatient with his slowness to act. We bombard heaven with passionate prayers and cries, complaining that he does nothing when we think he should have done something. When we don't see the desired outcomes of our labor, or the fruits of our ministry, we ask "Why?" Why did you not work? How come there are no signs of fruits, after the many years that I have served in this fellowship? We even doubt whether we should be serving at all and, even worse, we call into question God's call in our lives. And we lose our patience because we interpret God's slowness to act as his indifference, as meaning that he doesn't care.

My mentor said this to me: You have to pray for patience before you can remain faithful and steadfast, since patience is the gasoline that keeps the engine of faithfulness running. Just as the people of Israel through patience inherited the promises of God, so also we through patience remain steadfast and unwavering in our loyalty to God. It is through patience that faithfulness is guaranteed; and it is through faithfulness that we reach the end.

Mary Moffat, one of the early missionaries to Africa, labored among the primitive African tribes for 7 long years with no apparent results. However, she hung in there, serving laboriously and patiently. A friend from England wrote asking whether she needed anything. "Yes," she wrote back, "send me a communion set—cup and plate. We shall need them some day."

In those times, it took a year for her letter to reach England, and another year for the communion set to reach Africa. During that time, a breakthrough came. A group of Africans became Christians through Moffat's patience and faithful labor. The packet containing the communion set arrived exactly on time for the first communion service.

What is Christian faithfulness? It is a rooted conviction that God's time is:

(a) always the best time,

(b) the right time, and

(c) the only time. No one who stays committed to him will ever be disappointed.

He may delay in answering our requests, but as F. B. Meyer said it well: "God's delay is not his denial."

Faithfulness enables us to believe that God will make all things beautiful in his time. And with that conviction, no frustrations, setbacks or sufferings can deflect us from our Master's business, which alone is the main business.

Thirdly and finally, faithfulness is needed in our walk with God; this quality is required in our personal relationship with God.

Once you have entered into a true personal relationship with God, one of the first things to learn is how we can hold fast to the Lord and stay faithful to Him for the rest of our lives into eternity. There is no turning back—ever! But how can I remain loyal, faithful or truthful to my Lord? Here are two teachings that may help:

(i) *Faithfulness as attitude*, that I am sustained by God's faithfulness. I believe in the faithfulness of God, which is the basis of my faithfulness towards him, my perseverance, my steadfastness. God alone is faithful, not by a faithfulness he receives from others, but a faithfulness that he himself is. His name is "faithfulness and truth", through whose name I persevere.

This alone is the basis of the perseverance of the saints. It is a comforting doctrine, and I still believe it. The fact that I can still persevere is precisely because of his Name. I can persevere in my relationship with God because I know that, although I am faithless, he will remain faithful. His grip on me is stronger than my grip on him. I know my own wayward heart, a heart that is prone to wander—Lord, I feel it—and the frailties of people in general, I know very well that we can falter, fail, and fall. We can turn our backs on God in stubborn disobedience, but He will never, never turn his back on us, nor will he cast us out of his strong, everlasting arms.

The hymn writer was right to say: "He holds onto me, forever I know; he holds onto me, and never lets go; I am trusting in him; I am happy and free; for I know my Lord is holding onto me."

(ii) *Faithfulness as action*, that which is impinged on us. Yes, it is by his power that we are kept faithful, but do not forget the other side of the story: it is also our responsibility to be faithful. Not only is faithfulness an attitude, it is also an action. For there to be a continual, real, and deep relationship with God, faithfulness through action is required of us. However, we cannot achieve this alone.

Therefore St. Augustine said: "What he demands of you, he shall supply." When God demands faithfulness of us, he knows that we, by ourselves, can never fulfill his demands. Our faithfulness never measures up, and in fact is often a letdown. He knows that our faith is crummy, weak, and impure; if left alone, we are doomed to destruction and to forsaking Christ. But God does not leave us there, to our own devices; rather, He supplies us with the enabling Spirit, who works faith and faithfulness in us. It is by the power of the Spirit that we are able to persevere in our walk with him until the end of our life's journey. This explains what St. Augustine meant when he said: "What God demands of you, he shall supply." He enables you to fulfill the demands he places upon you. It is his power and our responsibility—the two work together. The Christian life is never passive, but always active if we truly love Christ.

He demands faithfulness of us, but at the same time he supplies the dynamism for it, i.e. the Holy Spirit, who creates in us the fruit of faithfulness. My first mentor, Henry Blackaby, emphasized: "If God saves me, and leaves me alone to fight the battle of the flesh, I would never want to be a Christian. Just as I am powerless in my salvation, so am I powerless in my sanctification." But knowing that we cannot do it on our own, he gives us dynamism in the gift of the Holy Spirit. A dynamic faith is indeed a possibility.

John Gladstone said: "Faithfulness can be within our reach, it can be our possession, our glory, and our wealth," if we are rooted in the Holy Spirit. Notice that the Spirit is the root, and faithfulness is the fruit. Being rooted in the Holy Spirit, Stephen was a man who was "full of faith."

This is the Good News: God did not save us to leave us alone to fight the battle of the flesh; he indwells us by the power of the Holy Spirit. Therefore we are able to remain strong and steady under the fierce winds of change, doubt, temptation, and bitter disappointment.

6

Polluted Well

(I Pet 2:1–3)[1]

A STORY is told in China. In a village, people yearned
for clean and pure water. Finally they discovered a
deep well from which they draw such water, creating happy
lives. One day the water from the well tasted terrible. Many
people became severely sick, and some died because of it. A
young man was determined to search and find out why the
water tasted so horrible. He therefore went to the bottom
of the well, and found a dead cat floating on the water. This
created misery in the village, because clean water is something that the people there cannot live without. The well
was contaminated and polluted. The diseases or germs that
resulted were contagious and destructive. They ultimately
brought about sicknesses and the deaths of many people in
that village.

This physical well makes me think analogically of the
spiritual well. Is your spiritual life polluted with diseases?
Are you aware of what any germs might do to you?

---

1. This sermon was frequently preached to young people in
Canada and abroad.

Listen to Peter's advice in I Pet 1:2, where he tells Christians to "strip off," "lay aside instantly," or "rid themselves of" these contagious germs. Not only are we to be aware of them, Peter emphatically stated that we ought to get rid of them as quickly as we would get rid of a garment if it were on fire. Peter's language communicates the severity, urgency, and danger of the issue.

In Peter's time, people tended to wear long, flowing robes. Suppose a man were to stand too close to a fire and suddenly discovers that his clothing is on fire, what would he do? Without hesitation, he would quickly strip it off and throw it aside. That is exactly what Peter wanted us to do, due to the severity and urgency; if it were left unattended, the calamity would be insurmountable. Peter exhorted us not to entertain germs, not to befriend them and not to let them pollute our spiritual wells. Get rid of these germs because they can cause us to lose our appetite for God's Word; they may also bring harm our Christian witness and growth; they may bring curses and damnation on our human relationships. This explains why Peter's language was so strong and emphatic: "get rid of" germs immediately.

Let us do some soul-searching and see if Peter was describing our spiritual situation, if our spiritual well is so polluted that immediate action must be taken to prevent curses and destruction. In verse 1, Peter mentioned five specific germs:

Firstly, strip off *all malice*. Malice involves a deep-seated hatred of others, with a deep, dark feeling of intense hostility. A malicious person is mean; he hates others to the point of hurting them; he is not satisfied until he makes others suffer. He is also someone who intentionally and joyfully wishes people harm and misfortune. Peter pleads with us to watch out, to get rid of this, because it might destroy us. Those who destroy others in their malice will end up destroying themselves.

Secondly, strip off *deceit*. This refers to someone who may be mentally brilliant, but who is socially unreasonable. It points to cunning, clever, and tricky practices. It refers to the clever manipulation of people to serve one's own ends. For example, an unscrupulous politician makes all kinds of pre-election promises in order to get people's votes, but never intends to keep them. Peter commands us, "get rid of it." Such deceit or double-talk should not be our practice. We should be open and our motives must be clean and transparent.

Thirdly, strip off *hypocrisy*. It is like an actor on the stage, acting out several roles, but none of them reflects his true self. However, one must not confuse hypocrisy with failure. A *failure* does not necessarily reflect a *hypocrite*. Someone may be very genuine both in motive and deed, really trying hard at something but failing. Most of us are genuine doers and lovers, but fail because we know how hard it is to satisfy expectations. C.S. Lewis said: "Those of us who think it is very easy to do good have never tried hard enough on it." The more you try to love, the more you feel how difficult it is to do it well. Concerning those who truly make every effort but fail, God understands our efforts and will continue to embrace us even in our failures. A genuine failure can be forgiven, and the person can be given a second chance. As Paul Tillich said, "He who tries and fails can be forgiven. But he who never tries and thus never fails is already a failure."

On the contrary, a hypocrite is someone who says something and then doesn't even try to do what he says, and yet can pretend to be other than what he really is. He does not practice what he preaches. Jesus rebuked the hypocrites. He plainly stated that they are "snakes, sons of vipers" (Matt 23:33). A contemporary writer, Thomas Carlyle, said something that might gladden the hearts of those who love beauty and cosmetics. Rather than opposing this, he commented: "You can take the most evil person, dress him up with fine clothing and cosmetics, and you can turn that person into a lady and a gentleman." What he implies is that a person may look like a millionaire on the outside, but can be utterly bankrupt on the inside; beauty on the outside, but beast on the inside. Peter encouraged us to do away with hypocrisy. Furthermore, we must stay away from a hypocrite, lest we also might become one.

Fourthly, strip off *envy*. Envy arises when others have greater talents or possessions than we do. It arises when others receive more honor than we do.

Once I was speaking to a group of teenagers. In a fit of rage, one teenage girl used an iron rod to hit her best friend, who later ended up being hospitalized for a week. I still remember how we talked for hours in a little room. I asked: "Why did you hit your best friend? She loves you, doesn't she?" Her reply sent a severe chill down my spine. "I hit her to hurt her because she is too beautiful; she is too good, and she has all the attention that I wish for myself. She has been the brain of the Sunday school class, and I cannot stand her being the center of attention." Then she looked away from me, hoping that I would not see the tears well up in her eyes.

There was a civil war raging within her heart. It was as explosive as the Vietnam War. Envy has broken friendships by the thousands. This is why people often call it the "green-eyed monster" or the "mental cancer." Prov 14:30 calls envy "the rottenness of the bones." Envy has corrosive effects upon our physical, emotional, and spiritual health.

Peter told us to get rid of envy because it destroys happiness; it disturbs our peace of mind; it keeps us awake at night; and it deprives us of common sense and vitality. As a result, we are not able to reach the potential that God intends for us. May I say this: one of the greatest victories that I have ever won is to be only what God configures and intends me to be. I reckon that others may be stronger and better in many ways than I am, and I praise God for them. Likewise I thank God that "I am myself," loved by God and used by him in unique and different ways. Whatever gifts we have, they come from the loving and wise heart of God. We are not held accountable for what we do not possess, but only for the gifts or opportunities that God has showered upon us. Every gift that we possess should be used for God in worship of him, and also used in the service of others.

Finally, away with *slander*. This is speaking evil of others in order to deface them. Slander may be unfounded gossip or a misrepresentation that is intended to defame and damage another's reputation.

A Sunday school teacher complained to me that the majority of the children chose to go to the other class, while only three registered for hers. "Well, the other teacher always brought cookies and candies to her class. She always told stupid stories, but I always taught the Bible. She has a way of manipulating the kids, but I am faithful to the Lord.

Even though only three came to my class, they are all very obedient and smart. Look at the kids in her class—they are noisy, naughty, and dumb." That is slander: attempting to discredit or belittle a co-worker. There is truth in the saying, "it takes little to belittle." By this, many lives are destroyed.

Since we have been born again (I Pet 1:23), since we have tasted the goodness of God (I Pet 2:3), let us therefore clean up our spiritual wells. Let us get rid of any germs that there may be in our lives. In verse 2, Peter writes that, since we have new life like "newborn babies," we should eagerly crave the pure milk of God's Word, through which we grow. By "newborn babies," Peter did not only mean new converts. He was talking about *a life-long attitude* that we must adopt, irrespective of age and circumstances, namely that of a newborn baby, craving, screaming and longing for milk, the very thing that our spiritual life cannot do without. No matter how old we are as believers, how long we have been in the ministry or how difficult our circumstances are, these things should not affect our child-like attitude, our constant and perpetual need of spiritual milk, the only necessity of our lives.

In the tropics of Central Africa, many people are afflicted by a disease called sleeping sickness. The disease is caused by a parasite that is carried by a tiny fly. When this fly bites a person, it transfers the parasite to him. Slowly, the parasite multiplies in the victim's blood. It is a painless disease that causes drowsiness, sleep, and eventually death. Gradually, the African government discovered that there was a close connection between the bite of the flies and certain death. Having known the cause, people began to clean up the areas around their homes; they cut down the jungle bushes; they sprayed the insects' breeding places and cleaned up the contaminated wells in their gardens. They thus created an environment where the flies could not thrive.

Sin is like the fly, spreading a disease that creates spiritual sleep and sickness. What is the remedy? In order to defeat sin, we must get rid of its breeding ground. We should create an environment of cleanliness for the soul by feeding on the pure milk of God's word. The flies of temptation and sin will not conquer you if you keep your spiritual well clean, and if you feed on God's holy word.

How do we approach life? Let us approach it as a screaming infant, yearning desperately for the milk we need. Let us not entertain sin, but fight against it by feeding on the Word of God. As D. L. Moody put it, "The Bible will keep you away from sin or sin will keep you away from the Bible." Take the attitude of the Psalmist, who declared:

Blessed is the person whose delight is in the law of the Lord, and on his law he mediates day and night. He is like a tree planted by streams of water which yield its fruits in season and whose leaf does not wither; whatever he does, he prospers" (Ps 1:3).

7

Reach the End, not the Top[1]

(PHIL 3:12–16)

THE AMERICAN politician Martin Luther King, Jr., once gave inspiring advice: "If you cannot fly, then run; if you cannot run, then walk; if you cannot walk, then crawl. By all means, move forward."

I believe that we can all agree with his wise words; even St. Paul would have no difficulty in accepting them. Paul, at the moment of writing Philippians, was in prison. There in a dark, dirty, and damp dungeon, he reflected about life and the purpose of God in his life. His resolution is stated clearly and plainly in verse 13: "This one thing I do, forgetting what is behind and straining toward what is ahead." Paul's aim is to press on, to march forward towards the end to which he was called.

I believe that this should be our aim also. We too should say, like St. Paul did: the one thing we will not do is stay where we are. We thank God for guiding us this far. As we seek to "live up to what we have already obtained," we will not stay where we are. We will march forward, press on

---

1. This sermon was preached in 2008, in the Community Chapel of the Tyndale University College and Seminary in Toronto.

to lay hold of Christ, and finish what we have begun. God never calls us to reach the top, but the end. But how can we press on till we reach the end?

This little section of Paul offers us four pointers:

Firstly, by a proper estimation of ourselves, which is Humility.

As Charles Spurgeon put it simply, "Humility is the right estimation of oneself." Augustine the theologian once said that if you were to ask him, "What is the first thing in religion? I would reply: the first, second, and third there is Humility."

Only a life that illustrates humility will press on towards its goal. Paul writes in verse 12: "Not that I have already arrived, not that I have been made perfect …" I still need to learn, to grow, and to know God. Did you notice Paul's humility? The hero of faith, the one who said, "for me to live is Christ, to die is gain," himself confessed that "I am not there yet; I need to know God." Because he needs God, he wants to grow and to press on.

Why do people not want to grow? Simply because they do not see the need. Only when you acknowledge how weak you are and how needy you are, will you want to grow. We sing the song, "The poor shall be made rich; the weak shall be made strong." But unless we confess our poverty and weakness, we will not press on and we will never experience the richness of God and the power of God.

Martin Luther put this aptly: "God created the world out of nothing, and as long as we confess we have nothing, God can make something out of us." That is humility—to confess our spiritual bankruptcy, that we are totally at the mercy and under the power of God. Only a church that acknowledges that she has no goodness and no wisdom of her own can draw nigh and lay hold of Christ and all his benefits.

The same principle applies to marriage. In 1984, on September 1, I was proudly wedded to my wife, and we have now celebrated our silver wedding anniversary. Prime Minister Steven Harper sent us a congratulatory note. Quite an encouragement!

I recalled that, on that day when we signed our lives away to each other, a beloved sister performed a solo. While the music was going on, I turned to my wife and said: "Ceceilia, from this day on, you need God." Do you know what she said to me? "From this day on, you need God more." I did not realize that she was a prophet. Indeed, I do need God more than her. However from the first day of our marriage, when the two of us walked down the aisle, we acknowledged this fact: "we are most needy of God all the more." A wedding certificate and a Prime Minister's certificate are memorable. But without God we can only maintain a marriage; with God, we can sustain it.

Secondly, by a "deliberate" forgetting of the things that hold you back (verse 13).

Paul said: "Forget what is behind." This is not just any forgetting, but a "deliberate" forgetting of the past. To be sure, there is nothing wrong with looking backwards, if this causes us to move forwards. If the past fortifies us to march forwards with diligence and intelligence, then remember it; if it mortifies us, robbing us of joy and vitality, then forget it.

There are things in the past that become hindrances to our pressing on. Let me name a few of them:

Don't look back at:

(1) sins that have been forgiven;

(2) the defeats that get you down;

(3) wrong decisions that cannot be changed;

(4) the old conflicts that only make you bitter towards others;

(5) the failures that send you down the corridor of despair. All of these things will hold us back, and we may end up hating God, hating others and even hating ourselves.

All of us have experienced failures of some sort. Failure should be recognized as a means to growth. I thank God for my failures, for through them I have learned three things:

(a) that God is faithful—that he has not forsaken me even when I fail him;

(b) something about myself—that I am a weak vessel in which a precious treasure dwells, and that he chooses to use me, even as a weak earthen vessel;

(c) how to minister better to my colleagues who struggle with the same failures that I have had.

(6) What about past victories? Oh yes, victories can hold us back, if we dwell on them and forget about our responsibilities ahead. The glories of our former days must not become substitutes for what should have been the glories of today and even tomorrow. There is always more to be done; more of God's grace available to us as we strive together. Don't live in your past achievements, as if it what is happening now does not

really matter. Don't dwell on your past glories, as if to say, 'it happened once, and that is enough.' That is a tragic existence—living as if God's grace is deficient, as if God is dead. No, God is fully alive; his grace never runs dry, and thus we should run to lay hold of its richness.

Thirdly, by a "conscious choice" of single-mindedness, focusing on Christ alone as the origin, motivation and goal of our spiritual growth.

Paul said: "This one thing I do" is to lay hold of Christ alone—his call, his voice, and his purpose, "the one who calls us heavenward, to win the prize for which we are called" (verse 14).

Soren Kierkegaard put this well: "The purity of heart is to will one thing" –to heed his voice, his call, and to press heavenward to grasp him and all the blessings that God has prepared in Christ. To be single-minded is to be Christ-minded. Double-mindedness cannot achieve anything, but shows impure motives, which are the cause of people's downfall.

To hear Christ's voice calling us is to be seized by [to lay hold of] him; and as we are seized by him in grace, we cannot help but seize him in return by faith.

When my boy nearly 3 years old, he learnt for the first time to run quickly in a gym, which was filled with kids and parents. I saw him at a distance and called out: "Hansel, daddy is here. Come to me." He heard my voice, and then he saw a toy in my hand. I shouted, "Come to daddy." In the midst of the noises, the voices, and the crowd, he:

(a) heard my voice, calling him forward;

(b) saw the toy; and

(c) ran as quickly as he could, totally oblivious of the commotion and distractions, only to receive the gift (toy). Not only did he receive the toy, he was also welcomed into his daddy's embrace. With excitement, he said: "Dad, next time when you come to pick me up, could you bring me a toy?" From that day, I never came empty-handed, but always had something in my pocket for my son.

John Calvin said: "When Christ comes to us, he never comes naked, but clothed with his gifts, benefits or blessings to bestow upon us." Not only is Christ the origin, he is also the goal of our Christian walk. He is the prize, the culminating point of our race. Like a runner, we reach for the finishing tape; we aim at one thing—the prize, Christ himself, the end to which we are called.

Just as my son ran towards me to lay hold of his daddy and all that his daddy represents or brings, so we too run heavenwards to fully enjoy him, for we can embrace many more blessings and gain much more knowledge of him. Not only should we be possessed by him, we must also possess him. To hear him is to heed to his voice; and to heed his voice is to be seized by him—Christ, the only one whose voice we must obey in life and death, because he is the inspiration, the goal, and the destination.

Finally, by a determined act of perseverance [verse 14).

Paul wrote: "I strained ahead . . ." This is a metaphor of a disciplined runner, striving and straining for the finishing line. As a teenager, I was a fast sprinter in the 100 meters.

I had my coach who trained me early each morning, who inculcated in me a determined act of perseverance.

What is the difference between a quitter and an achiever? A quitter quits a second too soon; an achiever hangs in there until the job is done. To persevere is to grow and to succeed. Alexander the Great was asked how he had conquered the world. He replied, "By not wavering." It was this steel-like tenacity that caused Athanasius to declare bravely against the heretics: "If all of this world falls from the truth, I will stand!" William Carey spent over forty years in Burma and India. When asked to explain his astonishing accomplishments, he simply answered: "Perseverance."

There are three things that are needed to accomplish any project:

(a) a dream;

(b) action; and

(c) perseverance. We need people who can dream, or we will never see our dreams come true. We need to turn our dreams into actions, and then undergird our actions with a determined act of perseverance. Without dreams, a campaign loses its direction and fire; without hard work or perseverance, a dream vanishes into thin air and the purpose sinks into nothingness. Therefore, persevere when misunderstandings or inconveniences occur, since perseverance will turn stumbling blocks into stepping blocks and will turn aspirations into achievements.

Robert Greenleaf said: "Behind every great achievement is a dreamer of great dreams." Paul would say that this is true, but insufficient. He would add: "Behind every great achievement is a dreamer *and* a disciplined perseverance."

So never give up; persevere and press on until you hear Christ's voice, the only voice that is most consoling to our hearts: "Well-done, thou good and faithful servant."

8

Jeremy's Egg[1]

(I Cor 15:12–19)

THE WRITER C. E. M. Joad once remarked, "If I could interview a personality of the past, I would pick none other than Jesus of Nazareth; and I would put to him 'the most important question in the world': 'Did you or did you not rise from the dead?'"

The fact of the resurrection is of paramount importance to the Christian faith. The belief that God raised Jesus by grace is not one of the many bricks in the structure of Christianity; rather it is the cornerstone, the foundation on which the whole edifice rests.

Deny the resurrection, and you will not have Christianity. Christianity stands or falls on this point. This is why St. Paul insisted in I Cor 15:12–19 that, if Christ has not risen, there would be several disastrous implications. Had Christ not risen, Paul reasoned:

(i) our preaching is useless;

(ii) our faith is vain;

1. This sermon was preached in the Easter Service of 2007 at the Wesley Methodist Church, my home church in Sibu, Sarawak, Malaysia.

(iii) the apostles were false witnesses;

(iv) we are still in our sins;

(v) those who have fallen asleep in Jesus are lost; and

(vi) Christians of all people are the most to be pitied because, without the empty tomb, there is no hope of New Life.

Easter is about New Life. The stone was moved. Why? Jesus did not move the stone so that he could get out of the grave, since he could have left it in any way he chose; he moved it so that we could get inside the tomb and see for ourselves that it is empty. Having seen it, the disciples shouted: "He is not there! He has risen indeed; the tomb was empty."

ILLUSTRATION

Ida Mae Kempel once wrote an article entitled, "What's in Jeremy's egg?"

Jeremy was born with a twisted body and a slow mind. He was still in the second grade at the age of 12, seemingly unable to learn. His teacher, Doris Miller, often became exasperated with him. He would squirm in his seat, drool, and make grunting noises in class. He was certainly an inconvenience to Miss Miller. She decided to send him away to a special school, and talked with Jeremy's parents about this.

Jeremy's mother cried softly into a tissue, while his father spoke. "Miss Miller," he said, "there is no such school nearby. It would be a terrible shock to Jeremy if he were taken out of this school, because he really likes it here.

Worse still, our only child has a terminal illness. Please let him stay here."

Later, as Miss Miller pondered the situation, guilt washed over her. "Oh, God," she prayed aloud, "here I am complaining when my problems are nothing compared to those of that poor family. Please help me to be more patient with Jeremy, the slow learner."

From that day on, she tried hard to ignore Jeremy's noises and his blank stares.

Then one day, he limped to her desk, dragging his crippled leg behind him. He told her, "I love you, Miss Miller." He said it loud enough that everybody in class could hear it.

When spring came, the children talked excitedly about Easter. Miss Miller told them the Easter story and then, to emphasize the idea of "New Life" springing forth, she gave each of the 19 children a large plastic egg.

"Now, I want you to take your egg home and bring it back tomorrow with something inside that indicates new life."

The next morning, 19 children came to school, laughing and talking as they placed their eggs in the large basket on Miss Miller's desk.

Miss Miller opened the first egg, in which she found a flower. "Oh yes, a flower is certainly a sign of new life," she said. "When plants peek through the ground, we know that spring is here." A little girl in the first row waved her arm and said: "That is my egg."

The next egg contained a plastic butterfly. "Oh yes, we all know that a caterpillar changes and grows into a beautiful butterfly. Yes, that is new life too." Little Judy smiled proudly and said: "Miss Miller, that one is mine."

Next, Miss Miller found a rock with moss on it. She explained that moss, too, showed new life.

Then Miss Miller opened another egg. She gasped. The egg was empty, without anything in it. "Surely this must be Jeremy's, " she thought, "and he cannot have understood my instructions? I wish I could have told his mother about what he needed to put in his egg. Unfortunately, I forgot."

Because she did not want to embarrass him, Miss Miller quietly set the egg aside and reached into the basket for another egg.

Suddenly, Jeremy spoke up. "Miss Miller, aren't you going to talk about my egg?"

Miss Miller replied nervously: "But Jeremy, your egg is empty. You were supposed to put something in it that shows new life."

Looking into the eyes of Miss Miller, Jeremy replied: "Yes, but Jesus' tomb was empty too."

Miss Miller asked him, "Do you know why the tomb was empty?"

"Oh yes. Jesus was killed, and was put in there. Then he was raised from the dead. That is why my egg is empty, because it talks about New Life, doesn't it?"

The recess bell rang. While the children were leaving the school yard, Miss Miller cried. The cold inside her melted away completely. One should never underestimate the brilliance of a seemingly slower learner, such as Jeremy.

Three months later, Jeremy died.

Those who came to pay their last respects at the funeral home were surprised to see 19 eggs on top of his casket.

All of them were empty, symbolizing New Life and Hope. Jeremy believed this, and he has New Life.

The doubting Thomas said: "He truly is risen, our Lord and Savior." Because of Christ's resurrection, death has no authority over Jeremy, nor over us. Jesus promised us: "Because I live, you will live also" (John 14:19).

In conclusion, what does Easter mean? I want to share four simple points:

(i) It means the funeral of death. The greatest funeral of all is not Jeremy's, nor yours or mine; it is the funeral of death. The resurrection marked the day when death died. Death has had its own funeral; it is defeated and buried. St. Paul asked, "Oh death, where is thy victor? Oh grave, where is thy sting?" (I Cor 15:55). Death has no authority over Jesus.

(ii) It means that we who are in Christ are the people of the future resurrection. Not only do we have a Savior who can help us now, we also have a Savior who will resurrect us. So when you read someday in the Toronto Newspapers that Dr. Dennis Ngien is dead, don't believe it. At that moment, he will be more alive than he is now; he will have been transformed, out of the old clay body into a body that is immortal—a body that death can never touch and that sin cannot taint; he will have a body fashioned like the glorious body of Jesus Christ. Because he lives, I too shall live forever.

(iii) Easter means that, at the end of our life's journey here, it is not Death who comes to snatch us away, but the risen Christ who comes to welcome us home. No one can snatch us out of the power of the Risen Christ, because he is "the resurrection and the life." While death dies because of Christ's resurrection, life lives on because of it. Inasmuch as we believe in "the death of death," we also believe in "the invincibility of life." Life is thus shown to be far more powerful than death.

(iv) Finally, Easter means that because Jesus lives, we can face tomorrow; and *not only* tomorrow, but even today, with all its pains and anxieties, because we have a living Savior who loves us, who walks with us, and who talks with us until our journey ends.

Thus we can shout as Paul did: "Thanks be to God, who gave us the victory through our Lord Jesus Christ!"

9

A New Heaven and New Earth

(Rev 21:1–22:6)

Rev 21 begins with the announcement that the present universe "had passed away." John wrote in verse
1: "Then I saw a new heaven and a new earth, for the first
heaven and first earth had passed away." By "passed away,"
he did not mean that the present heaven and earth is to be
annihilated, but rather renewed. The Greek word "new"
(verses 1, 5) means *new in character*. What is in view is not
the extinction of the present universe, but the renewal of it.
The present universe will not pass into non-existence, for
the new creation is not a creation *ex nihilo* (out of nothing),
but a renewal of the old. In the passing away of the old creation, all that has come from sin and from the curse shall be
done away with. In this way, the old things passed away.

When the Fall occurred, the creation suffered from
the same curse as individuals as a consequence of the fall
of creatures. Just as there is then a renewal of the individual
who is under sin, so there will be a renewal of the creation
that is under sin. No wonder, then, that Paul said in Rom
8:19–21 that the present creation yearns eagerly to be lib-
erated from the bondage of corruption and brought into

the glorious freedom of the children of God. Ireneaus understood this to mean: "This created order will be restored to its first condition and be made subject to righteousness without hindrances." Although the present creation shall pass away, it will not be annihilated. It will be destroyed by fire (cf. II Pet 3:10), and even fire does not annihilate but burns up. Just as you put a dirty coal in the furnace, liquefy it, and a beautiful diamond emerges, so the Lord will take the old creation, put it through fire, and ultimately make it into a new creation and a new earth.

The passing away of the old creation and the creation of the new may be compared to the resurrection of the body. There is some continuity between this present body and the new glorious body that we will have. Paul illustrates this in I Cor 15 by the example of a seed. When a seed is sown, it dies, and then rises as a plant. There is continuity between the seed that is sown and the plant that rises. You are looking at the same plant, which initially is a seed but ultimately blossoms as a beautiful plant. We are looking at a single identity, at continuity and correspondence between the present body that is decaying and dying, and the future body that will be a new, glorious, resurrected body. It is still this body, but nevertheless a new, glorious, resurrected body, totally rid of any impurities and the effects of original sin. Even as the old body is not annihilated in death, so it is with the old creation. Herman Hoeksema explained: "And even as the resurrection body is not an essentially new creation, so the renewal of the universe is not an essentially new creation, not a creation out of nothing, but a renewal."[1]

1. H. Hoeksema, *Behold He Cometh!* (Grand Rapids, Michigan: Reformed Free Publishing Association, 1969), 679.

Just as we pass from the curse through redemption to the resurrection of the body, so the present creation passes from the curse through renewal and ultimately to its own resurrection—a radical, complete transformation. The same procedure occurs; that curse-redemption-resurrection will be experienced by the creation as will by individuals. Just as my body will be placed in the grave, decay, and corrupt, and yet I look forward to the resurrection of the body, this body, but nevertheless a new body, so the creation will corrupt, undergo renewal, and ultimately experience its own resurrection. Just as there is continuity between the seed and the plant, so there is continuity between the Old Creation and New Creation.

In verse 2, the vision of the future unfolds. Here John describes how he "saw the Holy City, the new Jerusalem, coming down out of heaven from God, prepared as a bride beautifully adorned for her husband." Just as the new Creation is real, so this city is a real city. Characteristic of human cities is their failure, because God is forgotten. Thus we read that the "Great City of Babylon", the very embodiment of rebellion and immorality, is fallen. The author of the book of Hebrews said it rightly: For here there is no continuing city, but we seek one whose builder and maker is God (Cf. Heb 11:8–10). Twice, John writes that the city was "coming down out of heaven" (verses 2, 10). This means that the city is God's work, his new work, and his new creation. It is a gift of grace—something that we could not conceive or build ourselves. The eternal city is a Holy City, the New Jerusalem. It is a beautiful city, as beautiful as a bride on her wedding day. Jonathan Edwards commented: "The eternal embrace and eternal joys are found in the New Jerusalem.

The atoning blood that Christ offered on Calvary's cross has removed all hindrances to intimate union with him." The church as the bride of the Lamb, which we are, will enjoy his embrace in the New City. The New City is a place where the bride and her groom are united for life, where they enjoy each other in that eternal embrace, in the ultimate marriage supper of the Lamb.

In verse 3, the voice came from the throne, saying: "Now the tabernacle of God is amongst men, and he will dwell with them. They will be his people, and God himself will be with them and be their God." This is the real story of the Bible. Sin entered the Garden of Eden; fellowship with the divine was broken by the Fall, but was restored by the atoning sacrifice of the Lamb. What Christ accomplished at the cross now finds its completion in the New City. Remember this: the Lamb is mentioned seven times in this text. By the intervening sacrifice of Christ, the tabernacle of God was restored. And John saw this: that the dwelling of God is among them. This is the perfection of divine fellowship. The accomplishment of the atoning work now reaches its climax—God and people dwell together in a marvelous union, as a bride with her groom. "They shall be his people and God himself will be with them and be their God." This is the language of the covenant, and is used in the Abrahamic Covenant, the Davidic Covenant and the New Covenant. "We are his people; God is our God" is the story of the covenantal work of the Lord God. This is the climactic promise of the covenant that God made with us: "they shall be his people; He shall be their God." And the final consummation of the promise is found right here in the New Jerusalem, where there is the perfection of divine fellowship, represented by the tabernacle of God. The unfluctuating joys of the future are bound up in God's fulfillment of the ancient unconditional covenants—the Abrahamic, Davidic, and New Covenants. In the New City, we will enter into the perfection of divine communion. "We will be his; he will be our God."

The latter portion of verse 3 reads, "God himself will be with them and be their God." In the Greek text and other manuscripts, it reads differently: "God with them [Emmanuel] shall be their God." This is significant, because this shows the Christology to be found. When the angel announced that the Lord would be born of Mary, it was said that his name shall be called "Emmanuel—God with us." The name Emmanuel, prophesied in Is 7:14, exclusively referred to Jesus in the New Testament. Jesus is Emmanuel, God with us. In heaven, our Lord Jesus, whose bride I am, shall dwell with me and shall be my God. This is the Gospel; the greatest blessing of all is Emmanuel, God with us, now and forever. I shall be his bride, the wife of the lamb; he will be my groom, my husband. Heaven is not heaven if the groom is not there; it is not heaven if it is not the place where we enjoy the marriage union. The focus is Christ, our husband, the Lamb of God, whose name is Emmanuel, the one I long to see and to be with.

This is the way we should feel about heaven. Nothing can be compared with the consummation of the relationship that we will have with our Lord Jesus Christ, whose name is Emmanuel, who is our God. I like what D. L. Moody said, that when he entered heaven, he was going to spend 1,000 days at the feet of the Lord Jesus, and then he was going to ask: "Where is St. Paul?"

What does the perfection of the universe look like? John conveys Jesus' revelation of the future through a kaleidoscope of rich images and symbols. Negatively, there is no sea (v.1). The New Creation is new and fresh, which John saw completely new, totally devoid of the things of this present world that are under the influence of sin and curse. In that place, "there was no longer any sea" (verse 1b). In the biblical literature, "sea" is a reference to the forces of chaos, seen as a dangerous and destructive element in the old creation. Therefore, this does not mean that there will not be a sea in the New Universe. By contrast, the old sea, which is under the curse of sin, is no more—there will be no more tornadoes or earthquakes, leaving millions homeless and hopeless, no separation between nations and peoples. The old sea of the first heaven and the first earth, that which is under the bondage of corruption, shall be no more. There will be no more sea to cause chaos and separation in the new city. John understood this first-hand, as he was on the Isle of Patmos, separated by sea from the churches he loved.

Verse 4 says that there will be no more tears or death or mourning, or crying or pain, for the old order of things has passed away. In other words, the things that are of this sin-cursed world have passed away. In our society death reigns, but death is no more in the eternal state, for there will be life without death. No more sickness, no hospitals, and no funerals, for these things of the Old Creation are gone.

The One who was seated on the throne said: "I am making all things new" (verse 5). This is an attestation to the divinity of Christ, whose "words are trustworthy and true." Only God can make "all things new." This is a divine word and a divine work—making all things new:

a. On us, there is a new name;

b. In us, a new song;

c. Around us, a new Jerusalem;

d. Under us, a new earth;

e. Above us, a new heaven;

f. Before us, a new revelation of the never-ending love of God.

Verse 6 reads: "It is done", words reminiscent of Jesus' own words on the cross (cf. John 19:30), and they mark the completion of the great purpose of God. The cross as the ground of pardon for sin is completed by the One who is "the Alpha and Omega" (verse 6). The One who sits on the throne, Christ, who resides with his Father, is qualified to declare the end of redemptive history because he is "the Beginning and the End" (verse 6).

John heard God's voice assuring him that the thirsty here on earth would be satisfied in the New Creation, as they are promised free and abundant drink from "from the spring of the water of life" (verse 6b). To the believer, the one who "overcomes", God promises that "he will inherit all things; I shall be his God, and he shall be my son" (verse 7). In the book of Revelation, "my son" always refers to Jesus, and does so because of the messianic Psalm 2, verse 7, where God says of the King that, "You are my Son." Those who overcome will also be called "my son." This is God's way of saying that they share the same status before him as

His Beloved Son. In the New City, there are no other kinds of people besides those who overcome, the co-regents of the world with God; and like the eternal Son, they too inherit all things.

John then wrote of the character traits and behaviors that are inconsistent with the kingdom of God (verse 8). He listed them, beginning with the "cowardly" and ending with "all liars." Note that this is not a general condemnation of cowardice and lying. Rather, it speaks of those who habitually or continually over time prove that they are cowardly and liars. He mentioned "the unbelieving, the vile, the murderers, the sexually immoral, the sorcerers, the idolaters," regarding whom he saw a glimpse of their eternal destiny. Their place is one of torment in the lake of fire, which is "the second death," meaning that they are eternally banished from God's presence. They will not enter the New City because they turned their backs on the One who holds the keys to the future.

John was given a tour of the capital city of eternity. The angel said to him in v.9: "I will show you the bride, the wife of the lamb." The city is thus described as the "bride of the lamb." Why is this? Because it derives its character from its occupants, taking on the character of its inhabitants. The occupants of the city are together the eternal bride, now enlarged beyond the church to encompass all the redeemed of all the ages. The bride is firstly described as the church (Eph 5); as we continue to see the unfolding of the eschatological plan, the bride enlarges to include all the redeemed. Ultimately, all of the saints form the bride, joined together in the New Jerusalem, all living in the Father's house. The city is likened to a bride because the redeemed are forever united to

God and the Lamb. It is further described as "the wife of the lamb" because the marriage has now taken place (Rev 19:7).

In verse 9, John is carried away in the Spirit to "a great and high mountain" so that he could gain a clearer vision of the Holy City. Firstly, he was shown the general appearance. The most distinguishing feature of the Holy City is God's glory within. Heaven is where the glory of God is manifested, unlimited, and unconfined. The glory flashes from that city throughout all eternity. God's glory is who he is; it is simply the sum total of his attributes. When God manifests his invisible attributes, he does so as blazing light, as he did to Moses and the people of Israel. When God manifests his very self, the city shines with God's weighty character. The majesty and wonder of God's character is revealed.

"The city shone with the glory of God and its brilliance was like that of a very precious jewel" (verse 11). "Brilliance" is something in which light is concentrated and from which light emanates. The city is like a giant light bulb, with the brilliant light of God's glory flashing out of it, except that the light does not shine through the thin glass of a light bulb, but through "a very costly stone, as a stone of crystal-clear jasper." The city appears to be a gigantic translucent stone, a Jasper or diamond, very costly because it is crystal-clear and unblemished. The eternal city has virgin beauty like a pure diamond, refracting the brilliant blazing glory of God throughout the New Heaven and New Earth. It is comparatively greater than the Beijing Olympic spectacle, with blazing light shining out of the city.

The brilliance of the full manifestation of God's glory so permeates the city that verse 23 states that: "the city has no need of the sun or of the moon to shine on it, for the glory of God has illumined it." This does not mean that there is no sun or moon in heaven; rather John says that the city has no *need of the light* of the sun or moon to shine on it. When John saw the whole city radiating glory, he looked for the source of the light. Where did it come from? Not from the light of the sun or moon. The splendor and beauty of the city came from the Lamb, the Lamb who was slain. Thus John cried out in recognition: "Its lamp is the Lamb" (verse 23). The lamp that gives off luminosity in the new city is the crucified Savior. The New City radiates the glory of the Lamb. There is no higher affirmation of the person and work of Christ than this. In Rev 5, the Lamb stands at the very center as the One who sits on the throne. Here in Rev 21, he stands at the very center of everything as the source of the glory of God. "Jesus shines brighter and purer than all the angels heaven can boast."

Secondly, John was given a vision of the exterior design of the city (verses 12–21). Human language fails to describe fully the magnificence of heaven. The picture we see is one of symmetry, order, and balance, which reflect the mind of God. The scene is overwhelmingly impressive. The city is a place with dimensions. It had a great and high wall, with twelve gates, and with twelve angels who are attending to God's glory and serving His people (cf. Heb 1:14). Written on these gates are the names of the twelve tribes of Israel. This celebrates for all eternity God's covenantal relation with Israel, the people of the promises. The gates were arranged symmetrically: three gates on the East, three on the north, three gates on the south, and three on the west. This was how God had arranged the twelve tribes around the tabernacle (Num 2). The massive city wall was anchored by twelve foundation stones underneath, on which were written the names of the twelve apostles of the Lamb. These stones commemorate God's covenantal relationship with the church, of which the apostles are the foundation (Eph 2:20). The layout of the city illustrates God's favor on all the redeemed, both those under the old covenant and those under the new covenant.

Verse 15 refers to a measuring rod that God used to measure out the city, the gates, and the walls. The significance of the vision is that the city belongs to God, with him marking off the boundaries of that which is rightly his.

Let us examine what he found. "The city is laid out as a square . . . its length, width, and height are equal," 1,400 miles measured in all directions. This points to the vastness of the city, spacious enough for all the redeemed.

A square has two dimensions: length and width. But John saw length, width and height—three dimensions. From a square to a cube—what does this symbolize? John's first readers would have no problem with this, for in the Old Testament the Holy of Holies in the Temple is a cube, that sacred place where only the High Priest could enter, and he only once a year. This is borne out by I Kings 6:20: "And the inner sanctuary was twenty cubits in length, twenty cubits in width and twenty cubits in height." The New City is the Holy of Holies; the city is a reflection of the unspotted glory of God. The wall is approximately 72 yards thick [144 cubits], which symbolizes protection and security.

The wall is made of jasper; it is a translucent diamond wall. The city is pure gold, like "crystal clear glass." Why does it have to be clear? Because that city has one great purpose, which is to radiate the glory of God. Therefore it can have nothing blocking the brilliant, flashing color of gold, shining forth from the city. The foundation stones of the city wall are adorned with every kind of precious stone, twelve of these brightly colored stones, which John described in amazing detail in verses 19–20. These brightly-colored stones refract the glowing brilliance of God's glory into a multiplicity of colors. The city is one of lavish beauty, breathtaking beauty, a spectrum of dazzling colors flashing from the New City throughout all eternity. It is beauty beyond all description.

The twelve gates are pearly gates (verse 21). Each one of the gates is a single gigantic pearl, nearly 1,400 miles high. In the Bible, the pearl is the emblem of redemption. Our Lord Jesus used it in that sense (cf. Matt 13). Pearls originate through an especially strong secretion by a shellfish as a reaction against injury from without. When an inanimate object comes into the shellfish, a pearl is secreted as a result of the irritation. In this sense, it is the answer of the wounded life to injury from without. It thus forms an illustration of the cross of Christ. This pearl is a pearl of great price, because it is the pearl of redemption that Christ wrought for us. John Philips puts this well:

> All other precious gems are metals or stones, but a pearl is a gem formed within the oyster—the only one formed by living flesh. The humble oyster receives an irritation or a wound, and around the offending article that has penetrated and hurt it, the oyster builds a pearl. The pearl, we might say, is the answer of the oyster to that which injured it. The glory land is God's answer, in Christ, to wicked men who crucified heaven's

beloved and put Him to open shame. How like God it is to make the gates of New Jerusalem of pearl. The saints as they come and go will be forever reminded, as they pass the gates of glory, that access to God's home is only because of Calgary. Think of the size of these gates! Think of the supernatural pearls from which they are made! What gigantic suffering is symbolized by those gates of pearl! Throughout the endless ages we shall be reminded by those pearly gates of the immensity of the sufferings of Christ. Those pearls, hung eternally at the access routes to glory, will remind us forever of One who hung upon a tree and whose answer to those who injured Him was to invite them to share His Home.[2]

As I read this, the physical make-up described—the stones and gems of all colors, the walls, gates, streets, and the tree yielding fruits—all point to the creatureliness of heaven. Archbishop William Temple said that the Christian faith is most earthly, and it is the most materialistic of all faiths. G. E. Ladd wrote that the Bible "always places men and women on a *redeemed earth*, not in a *heavenly realm removed from earthly existence*." Darrel Johnson comments: "The destiny of God's people is *not to go to heaven*, as we often say, but to enter 'a new heaven and a new earth.'"[3] Our hope lies not in being freed from creatureliness, but freed from the sin that causes the decay of creatureliness. "John's heaven is no world-denying Nirvana."[4] Thus the Christian

2. J. Philips, *Exploring Revelation* (Chicago: Moody, 1987), 254.

3. D.W. Johnson, *Discipleship on the Edge* (Vancouver, BC: Regent College Publishing, 2004), 374.

4. Quoted in Johnson, *Discipleship on the Edge*, 374.

view of the future is not "other worldly," but "new worldly." God does not abandon his material creation in exchange for a purely spiritual state of affairs. A true Christian spirituality is not one that denigrates, negates or escapes the material condition. This is one of the implications of the incarnation—God assumes humanity and become what we are, flesh and blood, creaturely stuff.

In Rev 21:22–22:2, John is given a vision of the internal condition of the city, which displays two perfections. Firstly, there is a perfection of worship. John saw no temple. This is a figurative way of saying that our worship of God is a direct experience, unhindered and immediate. "There is no need of a temple there, for the Lord God the Almighty and the Lamb are its temple" (verse 22). Their blazing glory fills the New Jerusalem. God himself is the temple. Life there is worship, and worship there is life. We will be constantly in God's presence; there will never be a moment when we are not in perfect, holy communion with the Lord God Almighty and the Lamb. Thus there is no need to go to a temple, or a chapel, or a cathedral. What the angel shows John is that God's dwelling place is no longer an identifiable, separate space within the city. His dwelling place is the city itself; it is all Temple. We become the true worshippers that the Father has always sought. Worship is the constant occupation of the redeemed, for God is the very thing that really matters. There is no need, no occasion, for a special temple, for God himself is the temple of His people in Christ. It is in him that we live, move, and have our being.

Secondly, there is a perfection of divine knowledge. Here on earth, our knowledge of God is mediate, that is, it comes through earthly things. There is a reflection of the glory of God through the light of the sun and moon. But there we shall know God through Christ, the Lamb who was slain was its lamp—that which gave off light concerning the true nature of God (verse 23).

Verse 24 says: "The nations will *walk* by its light and the kings of the earth will bring their splendor into it." "Nations" refers to all people, not just the Gentile nations. All the activity is performed in the light of the city; all their deeds and conversation is motivated by their perfect knowledge of and fellowship with God through the Lamb. All participate in the light, that is Christ, and this time we will do all things right.

The kings and nations will surrender their glories and honor to the "king of kings" (cf. Ps 68:29); heaven is not organized into political sections. The character of heaven is communal and universal, a place where everybody belongs and no one is left out. There is no social ranking, for all are equal. And all are consumed with one thing: bringing glory to the King of kings. Verse 26 reads: "The glory and honor of the nations will be brought into it." All glories, even kingly glories, collapse or dissolve into the glory of God the Father and the Lord Jesus Christ. In the end, the only glory that remains belongs to God. All the honor and glory of the nations concentrates around Christ, and the fruit [rewards given back to God] of their labors is consecrated to the glory of God and the Lamb. All of these are of perfect service to God. Thus the distinction between the sacred and the secular is not found in heaven, for everything is done with the Glory of God as the ultimate aim.

"The city gates shall not be closed by day, and there shall be no night there" (verse 25). This does not mean that there is no representation of the glory of the night in the New City. The idea is that there will be no night for the redeemed, but only constant light, constant uninterrupted activity, and perfect rest from terror and danger. Whereas in the old city, the gates are shut at night for fear of an enemy, in the New City the gates will not be closed; instead there will be perfect rest, with total freedom of access and freedom from danger. Heaven is a place of eternal rest, safety, and refreshment with the Lamb as the light.

Heaven being a perfect place, verse 27 says: "Nothing impure, and no one who practices abomination and lying, shall ever enter but only those whose names are written in the Lamb's Book of life."

Then the angel shows John "a river of the water of life, as clear as crystal, flowing from the throne of God and of the Lamb, down the middle of the great street of the city" (Rev 22:1–2). Pure water flows tumbling down from God's throne to the middle of its path. This symbolizes the constant, pure, and unobstructed flow of everlasting life from God's throne to God's people. Christ is the fountain, the spring, and the source of eternal life. Then, on either side of the river stands "the tree of life," which, for the Jews, is a symbol of the blessing of eternal life. In heaven, God's provision of diversities and richness will be unceasing, as "the tree bears twelve kinds of fruit, yielding its fruit every month" (verse 3). "And the leaves of the tree were for the healing of the nations"—the word "healing" does not indicate healing of illness or injury, which are not present in heaven. It is better translated as "health-giving" or "therapeutic." The leaves of the tree are life-giving or health-sustaining, like super-Vitamins. This is a figurative way of saying that we will enjoy perpetual health. Life there will be fully invigorated, rich, and exciting.

Finally, the vision concludes with several wonderful privileges of the saints (verses 3–5). In heaven:

(i)   there "shall be no more curse"—a perfect environment without sin;

(ii) "but the throne of God and of the Lamb shall be in it"—perfect government;

(iii) "and His servants shall serve Him"—perfect service;

(iv) "they shall see His face,"—prefect communion.

No man has seen God at any time, but the day will come when we shall see Him face to face. To see God as sinner is to be consumed by his holy animosity towards us. No one in their naked self, without God's righteousness, can see God and live. But in him, and being clothed with Christ's holiness, we are able to see God and not die. We shall be engulfed in his presence, exposed to the full blaze of his eternal glory. We shall see his face, know his heart, and understand his works.

(v)   "and His name shall be on their foreheads,"—perfect belonging and resemblance;

(vi) "and there shall be no night there,"—perfect blessedness.

John repeats the description of heaven's magnificence—it is a glorious place, with the Lamb as the luminosity, the centerpiece of that diamond blazing glory of God. All our activities are performed in the light of the city. Our being, our well-being, and our activities are governed and animated by the Lamb whose perfect light is our sole guidance.

(vii)   "and they shall reign forever and ever,"—perfect reign and glory. Just as we reside with Christ on his throne, so we shall also preside with him. As God's beloved children, we shall reign with God the Father and the Lamb, Jesus Christ, throughout eternity.

Related to this presiding activity in the New City, will there be creativity? I think so, for God promises: "I am making all things new?" (verse 5). There is an ongoing, continual creative work of God stretching throughout eternity. Heaven is not just an Eternal Day Off. Dallas Willard, in his *Divine Conspiracy*, captures this well:

> We will not sit around looking at one another or at God for eternity but will join the eternal Logos, 'reign with him,' in the endlessly ongoing creative work of God. It is for this that we were individually intended, as both kings and priests . . . A place in God's creative work has been reserved for each one of us from before the beginnings of cosmic existence. His plan is for us to develop, as apprentices to Jesus, to the point where we can take our place in the ongoing creativity of the universe . . .[5]

So there will be vibrant growth and unceasing creativity as we reign with God. There is no suspension of works, either divine or human. God continues to work, making all things new. In addition, our work will not be suspended, for we will reign with him. Heaven is not an escape from the responsibilities of our heavenly citizenship; it is the inten-

5. D. Willard, *The Divine Conspiracy* (San Francisco: Harper, 1998), 378.

sification and healing of these responsibilities. In the praise and service of our triune God, there will always be new surprises and adventures as God's gift of life and love continues to unfold boundlessly, serving as leaves for the healing of our being and deeds. The rest and peace of eternal life is not an eternal sleep. There will be new creative responsibilities, unending discovery, and pure joy in our communion with the God who is making all things new. There will be divine commendations, as we will hear his sweet voice: "Well done, thou good and faithful servant." You will get better, sweeter, and cuter than before. Well done!

This is heaven. Heaven is God's dream for us. Let us lay hold of his words, for "they are trustworthy and true" (verse 6). Or rather, let his efficacious words lay hold of us so that heaven becomes our dream, as it is God's dream for us.

In Loving Memory of My Beloved Mother[1]

L ATE NOVEMBER, 2009, I returned from Canada to visit with my mom in Malaysia, not knowing that it would be the final time that I saw her and talked with her. She told me: "Son, next time we meet again, you will see me, but not hear me." So it was. She died peacefully early in the morning of March 06, 2010, when she faded into glory with a failing heart.

The following constitutes the last words that she shared with me, her baby boy.

HER PRAYER REQUEST: I AM READY AND WILLING TO GO HOME

On November 22nd, I was sitting by her bedside. I observed that her mind wandered, being preoccupied with a lot of things she wanted to share with me.

Firmly and eagerly, she said to me: "Son, please pray that God will send guardian angels to escort me home. I am ready and willing to go. God will hear and answer your prayer because you are his beloved servant. I am exhausted,

1. Some of the materials appeared in the Memorial Service for my mom, Madam Ngu Poh Teh, on March 10, held at Zion Methodist Church, her home church in Sibu, Sarawak, Malaysia.

and I have exhausted everybody who loves me. I know that love from my family abounds, but my strength is failing and I am incapable of receiving it. Many parts of my body, especially my feeble heart, are increasingly failing. Very soon your strength will fail also. I have gone through ups and downs, joys and sorrows. I am blessed with a large family, with many grandchildren, all of whom have loved me. I am very contented. It is about time for me to rest."

Holding her hands tightly and with heavy drops of tears in my eyes, I prayed that God would grant her wish. She prayed after me, word for word, that God would have mercy on her and receive her into heaven as soon as He saw fit. Mother and son were wrapped in an intimate embrace, but with an indescribable pain because we foreknew her imminent departure. We wept profusely together for almost an hour.

REPRESENT THE FAMILY AND SERVE AS PREACHER IN MY HEAVEN-GOING SERVICE

She continued: "When the final hour comes, please do not oblige your wife and son to return here, because the journey from Canada to Malaysia is too long. Ask her to take care of her widowed mother in Toronto. It will be enough if you come alone for my memorial service. You are to represent the family and to speak, and as professor and preacher, you are the one most qualified to speak. Also, people really like to hear you, so let them hear you in my heaven-going service, which I know will be crowded."

I replied to her: "Mom, I have preached in many funeral or memorial services. If yours were the next, it would be the 185th." She commented: "That is a lot. Obviously the Lord has equipped you for the task. Therefore you should do just fine in my memorial service. I know that you are a well-known three-point preacher. So let me offer you three points, which you are to bear in mind for your speech:

(a) when you speak in my heaven-going service, you must not sob, because we have cried enough. She knew that would I sob—nobody could understand me so well. This service is your only chance, she reminded me: don't blow it; do not cry; and speak clearly;

(b) you must dress differently, like a regular Sunday service preacher, because you are different from the rest. Your calling is to be a Professor of Theology and a Preacher of God's Word, the highest and noblest calling;

(c) offer words of thanksgiving, not more than fifteen minutes, and in three languages—Foochow, Mandarin, and English, so that all attendees will understand.

WORDS OF THANKSGIVING

Be sure to thank all ten children and their spouses for their unfailing care for me. Don't forget to mention the six married sisters, who take it in turn to care for me, despite their own family needs. Tell them that I appreciate their being so sacrificial and willing to walk with me through the difficult period of my illness. Remember to mention your second brother and sister-in-law, Daniel and Grace. Since the birth of their daughter May Ngieng Lin-Ling nearly 30 years ago, I have lived with them, without any thought of leaving them. Although I have given them a lot of heartaches and inconvenience, they were willing to bear with me. Esteem Daniel because he has assumed the headship and leadership of the whole family for many years, alongside his heavy and demanding political career. Indeed, he carries *Heavier Crosses* than most of us.

Don't forget the pastors and sisters from the Zion Methodist Church who visited me frequently, and who celebrated Holy Communion with me as often as I needed, the volunteers, the female choir, relatives, and friends who attend the service. Please thank my Foochow peers, with whom I hang out almost every evening in Rejang Park, for always being there for me.

MY CHILDHOOD EXPERIENCE: TRUE LOVE IS SUFFERING LOVE

Included in my funeral speech was this childhood experience that I had with my mom.[2] I asked her, "Mom, do you remember what happened when I was eight years old?" "Oh, yes. Your father died," she replied.

I recapped this experience in my last conversation with her, to assure her that she was irreplaceable.

She was deeply moved, hearing it from me:

"When I was aged eight, I lost my father to cancer. A week after his burial, I became severely ill. The pain in my body eventually paralyzed me. I still remember, as clearly as if it were yesterday, how my mother, who was 43 years

2. This childhood experience also appeared in the article, "The God Who Suffers," published in *Christianity Today* (Feb., 1997). Later the article was chosen as one of the most significant 13 articles, and posted on Christianity Today's 50th anniversary webpage.

old and newly widowed, cared for me. She did not discuss with me how I felt. Rather, instinctively, she took me into her arms and caressed my back with her gentle hands, reassuring me with words of comfort and love for me. I grew so sick that I was hospitalized. Since we lived in a remote village several miles from the hospital, my mother carried me on her back, walking powerfully, uphill and down. With tears streaming down her cheek, she said: 'Son, Daddy is not here. But Mommy is still here. Hang in there. We will make it to the hospital soon.' Both mom and I wept heavily until we reached the hospital."

This childhood experience confirmed in me that a love that does not suffer with the suffering of the beloved is not love at all. True love is suffering love. It was in my pain that my mom was most herself, most motherly. She was most herself not in power, but in weakness; not in pomposity, but in suffering. She could have done or been different, except that through her love she became wounded for me; a loving mom is at once a suffering mom.

REMEMBER ME BY GIVING

When she regained her composure, I asked her how I could continue her legacy of self-giving. Her answer was simple: "Love was not self-seeking, but self-giving. It is in learning to give that I will be kept perpetually alive in your hearts.

"Baby boy, do not forget your sisters and their husbands, and your sisters-in-law. Present a small gift to each on my behalf on the first anniversary of my death when you would gather for a family reunion. If the situation permits, visit the remaining family members in Foochow, China, and give them my blessings.

"In addition, find four needy women." "Why four?" I inquired. "Because I have four sons, whom I treasure, and you could remember me by giving to them in my stead."

"Why women?" She replied, "Because I am a woman who has gone through a lot, and I understand how women, young and old, think and feel. Women can be strong. If it is possible, choose non-Christian women preferably."

I asked with curiosity, "Why non-Christian?" "Because Christian women could find help more quickly from the church than non-Christians can, whose needs we must seek to identify so that we can meet them.

"Just give a small gift to assure them that real love does exist, and in giving, I will be kept alive in your hearts.

"First, find a young, unmarried, and needy woman. Give her a small gift, and tell her that life can be sweet, even when facing uncertainties and fears. I was only 15 years old when I was pre-arranged to be wedded to your father, who was 16 years older than me, and who I met for the first time in Malaysia. Just as I was given an extravagant wedding gift by a poor couple in China, so now I am passing this gift through you to another, as an added blessing to her family, also hoping that she will find a good mother-in-law and the right mate.

"Second, find a young widow, like me. I had just begun to know your father, with whom I spent 27 years. He left me all too soon, and I was left alone to take care of all our 10 children. Consumed by grief and pain, and a widow aged 43, I was determined to stay single and to invest the rest of my life in my 10 children. Despair was not an option; a determination to live is what a young widow must exhibit for the sake of her beloved children. More importantly, 'God is my everlasting help, who neither slumbers nor sleeps; the sun shall not hurt me by day, nor moon by night. The Lord shall protect me in my going and coming, from now till forever' (Ps 121).

"Third, find a divorcee, and offer her a small gift. Assure her that she is not a bad person, but had a bad experience. Tell her to be strong, and that she can do it. She can make her children stand tall by being there for them at every moment of their growth. Lead her to find love in God, since God's love is forever and unwavering, which is the source of our comfort and strength. Hopefully a little gift will send notes to her soul that someone does care.

"Finally, find a retiree of 65 years old, and encourage her to live graciously and die gratefully, so that people might know how precious and sweet life can be, if we hold onto a proper perspective of life. Worldly possessions are not everything; motherhood—learning to be a good mother, grandma and mother-in-law—matters most, for that is a lasting thing that people will remember and treasure. God shall establish the works of her hands and bring to fruition her labors.

"Scripture says, 'It is more blessed to give than to receive.' What legacy have I left behind?" With some regrets and humor, she said: "I do not claim to have achieved *a legacy of self-giving*, although I have aspired to be self-giving. Throughout the long and lonesome years, I have tried to put my whole family first. I have tried hard to be both 'father and mother' to my children. Son, I did not do a great job, did I? But I have tried *to give without setting condition; care without adding pressure; love without being possessive.*

My dearest son, be a channel of blessings to them, as you already are. I shall be glad in heaven when you practice greater self-giving. Aspire to achieve a legacy of self-giving, and with God's help, you will do much better than I. Rest assured that the shadows of your mother's love will forever follow you."

MY RESPONSE: MOM, I LOVE YOU AND I MISS YOU

My mom was no perfect saint. She did what she was able to do, putting the children and the needy first. Since her demise, I have been grieving, and at times I have felt very disintegrated and insecure. She was my safe harbor amidst life's turbulences. She is now heaven's gain, but our immense loss. Her request that I dress like a preacher as I delivered the final speech in her heaven-going service was a form of healing for me. For years I wondered whether I had embittered her by moving away from being a medical doctor to become a Professor of Theology and a Preacher of the Gospel. It was her sole dream that I should become a medical doctor, but I broke with her dream. However, God has another plan for me, which she now accepts. Furthermore, her dream to have at least one medical doctor from the Ngien family, although not fulfilled in me, has now been realized in Dr. Derek Ngieng Yang-Yang, her dear grandson, who was by her bedside a few months prior to her death. God has made all things beautiful.

May 09, 2010 was the first Mother's Day I had without my mother. Not being used to her absence, I lapsed several times into depression and insecurity. Memories of her are still very vivid in my heart. I frequently meet her in my dreams. I miss my mother's soft touch on my face, her cheer, her stern chastisement, her company over breakfast, a stroll with her to visit her friends, nights of solemn and enjoyable conversations, periodic prayers, and reciting the Lord's Prayer, I Cor 13 and Ps 121.

In particular, the memory of mom bearing my pain helps me to understand the true character of the God to whom we relate. It is in God's suffering for me where God is most himself: he is most divine or most Godlike not in majesty, but in humility; not in pomposity, but in suffering. What consolation would I have received if my mother had remained aloof from my suffering? Likewise, of what help to wounded people is a God who knows nothing of pain himself? The cross communicates a love that truly suffers, a God who really suffers for and with me. Her life was indeed a testimony to the triumph of Agape love of I Cor 13, the text I read to her by her bedside for four years.

On the Mother's Day, I could hear her voice as clearly as if she had spoken yesterday: "Son, I will be watching you from afar; I, your mom, remain forever your *biggest fan* in all your earthly endeavors. See you on the other shore of heaven where we will all reside forever. When you miss me, put on a pink shirt or tie; you look handsome in pink; also, Hansel-Timon, my grandson, was born and wrapped in a pink swaddling cloth [due to a lack of blue, because too many boys were born on that day]. Make me proud, as I have tried to make you and all my children stand tall."

All these fond memories, which I cannot live without, knit us together much closer than ever, even though she is now far away on the "other shore" of heaven.

Was it William Shakespeare who said, "The lips of a dying man seldom lie"? Her last words reflect the heart of my mom—a loving and giving heart. They are memorable and powerful. They create such immeasurable joy and certain hope in me that I cannot help but respond:

Mom, I love you; I miss you; I shall follow your example of self-giving, for you alone supersede all else in it. In God's eternal love, there is no eternal separation, but only *changed address*, from earth to heaven. See you in heaven some day.